Preventing coronary heart disease in primary care

The way forward

Report of an expert meeting

Edited by Imogen Sharp

National Heart Forum
Tavistock House South
Tavistock Square
London WC1H 9LG

London: HMSO

ISBN 0 11 322000 6

Other publications by the National Heart Forum:

Coronary heart disease prevention in undergraduate medical education
Coronary heart disease prevention: A catalogue of key resources
Coronary heart disease prevention: Action in the UK 1984–1987
Coronary heart disease: Are women special?
Directory of members
Food for children: Influencing choice and investing in health
Physical activity: An agenda for action
School Meals Assessment Pack

National Heart Forum
Tavistock House South
Tavistock Square
London WC1H 9LG

Registered Company Number: 2487644
Registered Charity Number: 803286
VAT Number: 564 6088 18

Report edited by Wordworks, London W4 2HY.

Acknowledgements

This report is based on an expert meeting on *Cardiovascular prevention in primary care: The way forwards?*, held at the King's Fund in November 1994. The National Heart Forum would like to thank all those who helped to organise and all those who participated in the expert meeting. Particular thanks are due to:

- The King's Fund for organising and hosting the expert meeting from which this report derives

- The Steering Group:
  Professor Desmond Julian, Chairman, National Heart Forum (Chair of the Steering Group)
  Dr Alistair Cameron, Senior Medical Officer, Primary Care, National Health Service Executive
  Dr Godfrey Fowler, Reader in General Practice, University of Oxford (OXCHECK)
  Ms Elaine Fullard, National Primary Care Facilitation Programme
  Dr Muir Gray, Director of Public Health, Oxford Regional Health Authority
  Professor Ann-Louise Kinmonth, Primary Care Medical Group, Southampton University (British Family Heart Study)
  Ms Jean O'Brien, Primary Care, National Health Service Executive
  Dr Vivienne Press, Senior Medical Officer, Health Promotion, Department of Health
  Ms Imogen Sharp, Director, National Heart Forum
  Ms Chris Shearin, Primary Care Group, King's Fund
  Ms Sue White, Primary Care, National Health Service Executive
  Professor David Wood, Honorary Consultant Cardiologist, National Heart and Lung Institute (British Family Heart Study)

- The National Health Service Executive for funding the expert meeting

- The British Heart Foundation for providing funding assistance for publication of this report

- All the speakers who contributed papers; the session chairs; the workshop leaders and rapporteurs; and all the other participants who contributed to the success of the expert meeting

- Rosie Leyden, Wordworks, for editorial and production work on the report.

Editorial Group

Professor Desmond Julian, Chairman, National Heart Forum (Chair of the Editorial Group)

Professor Klim McPherson, Professor of Public Health Epidemiology, Department of Public Health and Policy, London School of Hygiene and Tropical Medicine

Dr John Noakes, Royal College of General Practitioners

Ms Imogen Sharp, Director, National Heart Forum (Executive Editor)

Ms Chris Shearin, Primary Care Group, King's Fund

Editorial partners

National Heart Forum

The National Heart Forum (National Forum for Coronary Heart Disease Prevention) is an alliance of over 35 national organisations concerned with the prevention of coronary heart disease. Members represent the health services, professional bodies, consumer groups and voluntary organisations.

The mission of the National Heart Forum is to work with and through its members to achieve a reduction in coronary heart disease mortality and morbidity rates throughout the UK. It has four main objectives:

* to keep under review the activities of member organisations in the field of coronary heart disease prevention and disseminate findings

* to identify areas of consensus, issues of controversy, and needs for action in the field of coronary heart disease prevention

* to facilitate the coordination of activities between interested organisations in the field of coronary heart disease prevention

* to make recommendations where appropriate.

Member organisations

Action on Smoking and Health (ASH)
Anticipatory Care Teams (ACT)
Association for Public Health
Association of Facilitators in Primary Care
British Association for Cardiac Rehabilitation
British Cardiac Society
British Dietetic Association
British Heart Foundation
British Medical Association
British Nutrition Foundation
British Paediatric Association
Chartered Institute of Environmental Health

Consumers' Association
CORDA
Coronary Prevention Group
Faculty of Public Health Medicine
Family Heart Association
Health Education Authority
Health Promotion Agency for Northern Ireland
Health Promotion Wales
Health Visitors' Association
National Association of Governors and Managers
National Association of Health Authorities and Trusts
Northern Ireland Chest, Heart and Stroke Association
Royal College of General Practitioners
Royal College of Nursing
Royal College of Physicians of Edinburgh
Royal College of Physicians of London
Royal College of Surgeons of England
Royal Institute of Public Health and Hygiene
Royal Pharmaceutical Society of Great Britain
Society of Cardiothoracic Surgeons
Society of Health Education and Health Promotion Specialists
Society of Occupational Medicine
Sports Council
Trades Union Congress

Observers

Department of Health
Department of Health and Social Services, Northern Ireland
Medical Research Council
Ministry of Agriculture, Fisheries and Food
National Consumer Council
Scottish Consumer Council
Scottish Office, Home and Health Department
Welsh Office

In addition, a number of distinguished experts in the field have individual membership.

King's Fund

The King's Fund promotes good practice and quality improvement in health and social care, through grant-making, information provision, service and management development, policy analysis and audit.

British Heart Foundation

The British Heart Foundation is the leading heart research charity and plays a major role in the fight against heart disease. It raises funds:

- to support research into the causes, prevention, diagnosis and treatment of heart disease

- to inform the medical profession of advances in the prevention, diagnosis and treatment of heart disease, and to encourage discussion of current research

- to inform members of the public of the ways in which they may reduce the risk of heart disease.

Contents

Foreword

The primary care team has an important role in the prevention of coronary heart disease, a role which the government has acknowledged both in formulating the new contract for general practice and the health promotion banding system, and in the national health strategies, including *The Health of the Nation*.

As part of the quest to find the most effective role for primary care teams, the OXCHECK Study and British Family Heart Study both set out to determine the effectiveness of nurse-conducted health checks, screening and lifestyle counselling in primary care, in changing coronary risk factors. Publication of the apparently disappointing results led to questioning about the potential of health promotion interventions in primary care, and the appropriateness of the current strategy. Because of the concerns, it was decided to convene an expert meeting of over 80 health professionals from a wide range of disciplines, to discuss the issues. The meeting was held under the auspices of the King's Fund, supported by the National Health Service Executive, in London in November 1994.

The aim of the meeting was to use the studies as a springboard for the future, drawing out the lessons learned, and considering the implications of existing evidence for policy and practice. Taking stock of what is known inevitably means also considering what is not known, and the research agenda. Several critiques and papers were prepared in advance, to stimulate discussion, and many different issues were addressed. Among these were: Were the interventions used in the two studies optimal? Can such initiatives in primary care be effective unless they are supported by more general health promotion strategies? What are the roles of different health professionals? To what extent do behavioural change factors need be taken into account? Should primary care regard prevention in those with established coronary heart disease rather than primary prevention as its first priority in this area?

While many of the questions remain unanswered, it was concluded that the studies showed a worthwhile short-term benefit at least. Different approaches need to be explored in primary care practice. Research on more effective measures of health promotion is also urgently needed, to lay the foundations for the policy and practice of the future.

We hope that this report of the expert meeting, generously funded by the British Heart Foundation, will contribute to a better appreciation of the potential of primary care in the prevention of coronary heart disease, and stimulate further action and discussion.

Professor Desmond Julian CBE MD FRCP
Chairman, National Heart Forum
Chair of the Expert Meeting Steering Group and Editorial Group

Chapter I

The way forward: summary and conclusions

The publication of the OXCHECK Study[1] and the British Family Heart Study[2] in 1994 generated much media attention and led to renewed professional debate about the role of the primary care team in coronary heart disease (CHD) prevention. Set in the context of the obligations of the GP contract and the health promotion banding system, the studies spurred discussion and concern about the effectiveness of a national policy measure that forms a central plank of the government's stated commitment to promoting better health: the role of the primary care team in health promotion and CHD prevention.

Cardiovascular prevention in primary care: The way forwards? was an expert meeting held in order to explore the implications of the studies, and to learn from them for future practice, policy and research. The conclusions set out in this chapter emerged during the discussions at the expert meeting. Their purpose is to help bring about an improvement in health promotion in primary care.

The studies add much needed evidence to a paucity of data, and show that health checks conducted by nurses in primary care can be effective in reducing coronary risk factors. Both interventions produced a small but worthwhile benefit, and led to declines in cholesterol and blood pressure levels among men and women. They were unsuccessful, however, in reducing smoking rates.

There is reason for optimism. Across the UK population, the public health benefits of the apparently modest effects could be significant, especially if they are maintained or accumulated over time. Later results indicate that they may be.[3] A potential 8% decline in coronary risk estimated from the risk factor reductions is encouraging, when applied to the whole UK population, and as effective as some population intervention strategies. These overall public health benefits may have been misjudged when the studies were first published, with expectations unrealistically high.

Health promotion is an essential and integral part of primary care in preventing CHD. But if it is to be effective, changes in current practice will need to be made. Although both study interventions superficially reflected the contractual health promotion obligations in primary care, they were substantially more resource intensive than current practice. More emphasis will need to be placed on improving the quality of interventions, including follow-up, and less on collecting data. Other types of intervention may be more effective, and priorities will need to be set - a point reinforced by the economic evaluation.[4] Primary care will also need a wide range of support, including training in both behavioural change and organisational development, backed by coherent national health policy. And a complementary research programme will be needed, in which ideas are developed and tested using expertise from a range of different social and biomedical disciplines.

The issue to be addressed now is not, 'Does primary health care have a role in reducing coronary risk?' but, 'How can health promotion interventions in primary care be made most effective?'

A public health strategy

Coronary heart disease is the leading cause of death in the UK, and a major cause of disability, but most coronary events in the population occur among those with moderate or low levels of risk factors. A multifactorial, population approach is needed to reduce the high rates of CHD in the UK, addressing the needs of different social groups and involving agencies beyond the NHS, to complement any strategies in primary care. CHD is a key area in the four national health strategies, which provide an important focus.

1   **Health promotion in primary health care needs to be part of a national, integrated strategy to reduce coronary risk, and should be supported by public health policy measures.**

    Although health promotion in primary care is an essential and integral part of any strategy to reduce coronary risk in the UK, it needs to be supported by wider, population preventive strategies and interventions. Primary health care teams do not work in isolation. Government policies which create a health promoting environment are needed - both nationally and locally - to support interventions in primary care. The conflicting policies of government make it difficult for primary care teams to reconcile the explicit goals of the health strategies and the health promotion obligations of the GP contract with, for example, lack of government support for a ban on tobacco advertising, and inadequate food labelling legislation. Policies to control tobacco use, to improve access to nutritious food, and to encourage physically active lifestyles may have a greater impact on behaviour change in the population as a whole, than health advice in primary care.

2   **Local health purchasers and commissioners need to adopt locality approaches to purchasing for health promotion, which include both primary care and wider public health measures.**

At a local level, health promotion in primary care needs to be set in the context of an overall district strategy, which encompasses those who do not attend health checks in primary care. An integrated approach to commissioning and purchasing is needed, including closer links between public health, primary care, and health authorities, and reaching beyond the NHS. Health authorities have been slow to support initiatives in primary care, but innovative approaches to local commissioning and contracting, which include primary care organisations, need to be tried. Commissioners of primary care also need to be able to draw up locally agreed health promotion contracts and select providers, using the contracting process as a vehicle for change. Involving GPs in commissioning is also important.

Commissioning needs to be based on local needs assessment, taking into account the social class and ethnic patterns of CHD, and the higher rates in deprived groups. The role and functions of public health need to be reassessed as a community resource, so that independent public health advice is available to inform primary care practice.

3   **Primary care teams need to work with other local services and organisations to develop health promotion strategies for their practice population, using a community-based approach to health promotion.**

Complementary population and high-risk health promotion strategies are important at local level. Primary care teams will need to form local health alliances to develop and implement locality-based health promotion strategies, and to ensure a coordinated approach. Local partners might include public health, health promotion departments, local authorities, schools, community nursing, hospitals and trusts, and environmental health, for example. It may be appropriate to adopt a community-based approach to health promotion, which includes community participation, addresses the needs of different social groups, and reaches those who would not be included in the GP health promotion contract requirements, such as children. In particular, primary care teams and public health professionals will need to develop closer links.

Policy

4 **Within the GP health promotion contract, the banding system needs to be amended, in order to provide financial reward for appropriate action, including high quality interventions, audit-based activity, and follow-up of patients, rather than simply data collection. It also needs to allow for and encourage local flexibility in setting priorities, rather than encouraging population coverage.**

The banding system currently provides financial reward for data collection and returning screening figures, rather than for quality health promotion interventions in the context of a risk-related strategy, and it provides no financial incentive for follow-up.

There will need to be a restructuring of how health promotion in primary care is resourced and rewarded, to change practice. The payment system will need to be reconsidered and modified, in order to encourage primary care practices to develop and implement an evidence-based strategy for health promotion interventions, with priority groups for targeting, and including intervention and follow-up (see 7 and 8). It should allow scope for innovation in primary care practice. It should also encourage primary care teams to work with others to develop a population approach to prevention for those with low and moderate levels of risk factors (see 3).

Furthermore, although teamwork in primary care is important in health promotion, the payment system does not encourage this. Methods of rewarding the whole practice team need to be addressed.

5 **The amount of data that practices have to collect should be reduced. The emphasis should be shifted to maximising the quality of data, and to using practice data for local needs assessment, targeting interventions and informing action, within both the practice and the locality.** *(See footnote on next page.)*

The GP contract and banding system, and the current monitoring system, place much emphasis on data collection, which is not the best means of measuring performance or of accountability. The quantity of data collected - simply to meet the conditions of the contract - is contributing to low morale in primary care, and may be a constraint to health promotion activity.*

Data that are collected should be manageable, relevant and useful to those collecting it, and compatible with other data sets. Such data should be used to inform health promotion practice and to improve the provision of services, including local needs assessment, setting priorities and targeting interventions, and monitoring activity. Feedback of information, by FHSAs and as part of audit-based performance review, is important to encourage change. Practice data should also be aggregated, to inform the development of local public health strategies, with help from public health departments (see 3).

To assist this, there is an urgent need for standardisation of data and definitions, such as hypertension. The requirement to collect routine data on body mass index should also be reconsidered. Skills and systems for data collection and use will also need to be developed both nationally and locally, and this may require training support (see 12).

6   **There is a need for a substantial investment of resources in order to develop effective health promotion in primary care. In the context of a primary care led NHS, this might be achieved through a shift in resources from secondary care to primary care.**
    Both the OXCHECK Study and British Family Heart Study achieved changes in coronary risk factors with substantial resources. However, it would not be possible to sustain such intensity of intervention in primary care practice on a day-to-day basis without additional resources. In order to achieve similar results on a wide scale, a substantial investment of resources is needed, including staffing, information technology and support, and education and training.

Since the expert meeting, and partly in response to it, the Secretary of State for Health has agreed to reduce the data collection requirements for the health promotion programme from 112 items of information, to eight items, and to further consider the annual reporting requirements and data collection. The eight data items include the numbers of those aged 15-74 who are: smokers, patients whose blood pressure has been recorded, patients with CHD, patients who have had a stroke/ transient ischaemic attack, obese patients, patients with alcohol intake above recommended limits, and patients with a family history of stroke/CHD.

There is a need for investment in organisational development for primary health care, and support to develop organisational structures and systems locally, to ensure that an average primary care organisation can deliver an effective health promotion strategy. National policy guidance will also be needed on organisational structures and systems, including data collection, and on health promotion interventions and priorities.

There might be a minimum specified amount that should be spent on health promotion. A substantial shift from secondary to primary care may be needed. Public health activity in health authorities could assist this in the context of a primary health care led NHS.

Practice

7 **Each primary care team needs to develop a health promotion strategy, with practice guidelines, based on research evidence of effectiveness, taking into account team roles and cost-effectiveness of interventions, and specifying priority groups. The flexibility in the health promotion banding system needs to be fully used, and encouraged through the FHSA approval process.**

There is a need for agreed practice protocols based on current evidence, to deal with all groups, including those at high, moderate and low risk of CHD, using the flexibility within the banding system. One person in the practice should take the lead responsibility to develop such a strategy.

Resources should be invested in strategies known to be effective, and sustainable in the long term. The OXCHECK Study and British Family Heart Study used specific multifactorial interventions: other strategies might be more effective. For example, interventions which tackle only single risk factors can be more effective, particularly in reducing smoking rates. Health promotion advice may need to concentrate on a few simple messages, rather than tackling too many risk factors at once.

Effective teamworking, with defined roles and harnessing the skills of different team members, is also important, and needs to be encouraged and supported. Training and motivation will need to be addressed (see 12 and 13). There will also be a need for clear definitions of responsibility and good coordination as primary care teams evolve and grow.

8 **Health promotion interventions in primary care need to use behaviour change models and techniques, and take into account patients' readiness to change behaviour.**

Health promotion practice in primary care needs to be informed by existing evidence on behaviour change. The interventions needed to change behaviour will be different for individuals at different stages of change (see Chapter 3). Changing health behaviour is both complex and resource intensive, and primary care teams, and others, need to have realistic expectations of the change that it is possible to achieve with health promotion interventions. Furthermore, since individuals' responses to health messages depend on their particular stage of change, it is important to use appropriate outcome measures, based on stages of change models, in evaluation and monitoring (see also 15). Intervention trials which ignore these considerations and fail to demonstrate effectiveness may be misleading.

9   **Primary care teams need to prioritise resources and focus health promotion interventions and follow-up on those at highest risk of CHD.**

With finite resources, primary care teams cannot provide effective CHD prevention interventions for the whole practice population, and resources should be invested in targeted strategies.

The priority in primary care should be to target effective interventions and follow-up towards those at highest risk of CHD, such as those with hypertension, diabetes, and established CHD, although population screening will be needed to identify these groups. However, as both the OXCHECK Study and the British Family Heart Study interventions showed, achieving the greater reductions in risk factors in high-risk groups required more intense interventions, with more frequent follow-up. Importantly, CHD risk may be highest among those least likely to attend health checks, and this will need to be addressed.

Complementary high-risk and population approaches to CHD prevention are important, particularly since most CHD events are among people with low levels of risk factors (see 3).

10 **The implementation of preventive measures in patients with established CHD, including coordination and follow-up, should be a very high priority within primary care.**

There is a high prevalence of CHD in the UK population, and preventive measures in patients with established CHD could have a substantial impact on total CHD deaths. However, there is a need to improve the management of patients with existing CHD: established, effective prevention measures are not currently systematically implemented. The primary care team could have an important role in improving prognosis, through improved diagnosis, management, and coordination of secondary prevention and follow-up of patients. For example, there are many unrecognised cases of CHD within the community - especially among women. Furthermore, follow-up of patients with existing CHD is often inadequate, affecting adherence to treatment and rehabilitation. GPs could have an important role in improving coordination between hospitals and primary care in the period immediately after patients leave hospital, and in follow-up.

11 **There is a need for explicit professional guidance about health promotion advice in primary care, by professional bodies, to help build commitment among primary care professionals.**

The attitudes and behaviour of health professionals towards health promotion and health education are important, but may be problematic. Primary care team members are perceived as an important and reliable source of health advice. However, GPs need to be convinced that the health promotion interventions are valuable: health promotion advice will be more effective if given by a professional who believes in it. Health professionals also provide important role models in health behaviour.

This could be addressed in both basic and post-basic training, using evidence-based research. The traditional orientation of the health services towards treatment means that many primary care professionals do not regard health promotion and disease prevention as their vocation. This may be addressed by implementation of the 1993 General Medical Council recommendations, and Project 2000, which give higher priority to public health.

Training support

12 **There is a need for training support for primary health care teams and FHSAs on health promotion strategies and methods and on organisational development.**

In particular, primary care team members who are planning, implementing and monitoring the practice's strategy for health promotion or giving health promotion advice need an agreed level of training in health promotion. Many of those undertaking health promotion work have no training in health promotion or screening. Primary care teams could be required to complete an assessed training programme.

For example, there is a need for further training for primary care on effective preventive interventions in primary care and populations, behavioural change models, communication skills, management information systems, and on the handling, interpretation and use of health and screening data.

Health promotion teaching should be included in the basic, post-basic (vocational and higher professional) and continuing education of all primary health care professionals including, for example, doctors, nurses, pharmacists, dentists, and professions allied to medicine. The health promotion knowledge and skills of primary care professionals should also be regularly updated. Professional organisations and educational bodies have an important role to play. The implementation of effective interventions in health promotion, particularly in secondary prevention, might be a subject for Medical Audit Advisory Groups (MAAGs) or their successors, to address.

13 There is a need for multidisciplinary training on health promotion for primary health care professionals, to encourage teamworking and the development of integrated services.

Training needs to be organised in multi-professional groups, as well as for single professional groups. Joint training across the primary care team, and across primary health care, FHSAs, community services and public health might be undertaken, for example, in order to assist teamworking and promote the development of integrated services. Access to public health expertise could also assist primary care teams with handling and interpretation of health promotion data.

Research

Many health promotion interventions in primary care have been poorly evaluated. In the early 1990s there was a paucity of research into health promotion in primary care. The OXCHECK Study and the British Family Heart Study have made an important contribution but more research is still needed. Further experimental research is needed to refine interventions.

14 There is a need for research to evaluate different types of practical health promotion interventions in primary care, to establish the important and effective elements in the intervention process.

Research is needed to identify effective preventive interventions which can be implemented in primary care, including effective methods of changing health behaviour. Realistic and practical interventions need to be evaluated. Health service managers should be involved in the design of such studies, to help shape pragmatic interventions which can be tested in practice.

In particular, research is needed on:
– the most effective teamwork models in primary care, including best use of the skills and strengths of different primary health care team members (eg GP, nurse, dietitian, health visitor, facilitator)
– the effectiveness of interventions by different primary care team members
– the effectiveness of different methods of giving preventive advice
– the optimal time periods for health checks, advice and follow-up
– individual and family approaches in health promotion
– opportunistic approaches and mass screening programmes
– factors affecting participation and non-participation in health checks
– interventions to reach those least likely to attend health checks
– the harmful effects of screening, such as anxiety, and whether the health gains outweigh these effects
– the effectiveness of interventions to change health behaviour in patients with existing CHD
– the interactions between type of interventions, patient characteristics and effectiveness.

Studies on the effectiveness of public health and community interventions in populations, including interventions among young people, and on the interactions between primary care and population interventions, are also needed.

Preventive interventions are very difficult to evaluate. Although randomised controlled trials (RCTs) are one of the most important methods in clinical research, they are limited in evaluating the health promotion intervention process. (Problems include contamination from the intervention group to controls and from other prevention messages in the community, confounding factors, and the long time lag before the impact of policies and preventive interventions is seen.) While rigorous scientific evaluation is essential, it is inappropriate to assess interventions for prevention and health promotion by uncritically applying the methods used to assess treatment.

Different types of research methodology need to be used, including qualitative methods, to assess the important elements in the intervention process. RCTs and observational studies might be combined or carried out in tandem. Follow-up time needs to take account of the time lag, and assess whether changes are sustained over time.

15 **Research on health promotion interventions in primary care should be multidisciplinary, with input from social as well as biomedical scientists, and should incorporate theories and models of behavioural change.**

Research on health promotion interventions in primary care often neglects available theory and evidence on health-related behaviour change. There is a need for behavioural sciences to inform the design of interventions and studies into health-related behaviour change. An approach which incorporates the expertise and perspectives of different social science disciplines, such as psychology, sociology and anthropology, as well as nursing and medical expertise, could be used. Risk factor outcome measures alone are inappropriate: evaluations need to measure individuals' readiness to change their health behaviour and assess the extent to which interventions move people through different stages of behaviour change.

Research on health-related behaviour change also needs to be made more widely accessible, by behavioural scientists, medical journals and professional medical and nursing organisations, so that available evidence informs health promotion interventions. Behavioural methodologies and models have not permeated the medical literature and currently do not always inform the practice of health professionals in primary care.

16 **Economic evaluation needs to be an integral part of studies on health promotion in primary care, and inform the conclusions of such studies.**

Cost-effectiveness and cost-benefit analyses need to be integrated into studies on preventive interventions in primary care, to determine whether the effects justify the resource input. The policy implications, including resource implications, should be addressed in any conclusions or discussion of the study results. Economic evaluation methods may need to be developed in order to assess accurately the costs of interventions to patients - including, for example, time spent in attending health checks and the economic costs of modifying the diet - as well as costs to the health service.

17 **In designing studies on health promotion in primary care, researchers should specify at the outset the expectations of the study and the criteria for success, and results should be reviewed objectively before dissemination. Dissemination of results also needs to be built into the design and funding of such studies.**

In order to help avoid bias in the interpretation of research results, it is important for researchers to specify before the study begins what would constitute a 'finding of significance' or a 'clinically significant outcome'.

To assist this, and help ensure that expectations are realistic, researchers and research funders could ensure that all new large trials include a systematic review of previous studies, which takes account of available literature in relevant fields, including behavioural sciences. Funding bodies might also ensure that those reviewing grant applications include representatives of all relevant disciplines; the same principle should apply in peer review of journal articles.

Interventions need to be not only well designed, but also well described. A strategy for effective dissemination of research results should also be incorporated in the design of studies on health promotion. Feedback of research results to health professionals is vital, but this communication needs to be carefully managed, to help avoid media sensationalism, which can have an important impact on the motivation of health professionals whose work it involves. Any dissemination strategy needs to include briefing of journalists as well as health professionals.

References

1   Imperial Cancer Research Fund OXCHECK Study Group. 1994. Effectiveness of health checks conducted by nurses in primary care: results of the OXCHECK Study after one year. *British Medical Journal*; 308: 308-312.

2   Wood DA, Kinmonth AL, Pyke SDM, Thompson SG on behalf of the Family Heart Study Group. 1994. A randomised controlled trial evaluating cardiovascular screening and intervention in general practice: principal results of the British Family Heart Study. *British Medical Journal*; 308: 313-320.

3   Imperial Cancer Research Fund OXCHECK Study Group. 1995. Effectiveness of health checks conducted by nurses in primary care: final results of the OXCHECK Study. *British Medical Journal*; 310: 1099-1104.

4   Field K, Thorogood M, Silagy C, Normand C, O'Neil C, Muir J. 1995. Strategies for coronary risk factor prevention in primary care: which is most cost effective? *British Medical Journal*; 310: 1109-1112.

Coronary heart disease prevention in primary care: two studies

The OXCHECK Study

Dr Godfrey Fowler, on behalf of the OXCHECK Team

Imperial Cancer Research Fund General Practice Research Group, Department of Public Health and Primary Care, University of Oxford

The origins of the study

The introduction in the mid-1960s of the Charter for General Practice, with its financial incentives for improved practice premises and for the employment of practice staff, including nurses, signalled major changes in the delivery of primary care in the UK. Gradually, a more proactive approach developed, with practice nurses taking on some of the preventive tasks which were a natural consequence of a more 'anticipatory care' philosophy.

In the early 1980s, the Royal College of General Practitioners published a series of reports on health and prevention in primary care. One of these reports, *Prevention of Arterial Disease in General Practice*, concluded that "about half of all strokes and a quarter of deaths from coronary heart disease in people under 70 are probably preventable by the application of existing knowledge".[1] It recommended that GPs should give priority to action to improve control of known hypertensives and diabetics, and to an active case-finding approach for detection and management of other cardiovascular risk factors.

As a first step, improvement in ascertainment of risk factors was called for, to achieve, in patients under 65 years, at least every five years:
- a recording of blood pressure, with treatment if this was ≥180/105
- recording of smoking behaviour, with help for those wanting to stop
- weighing of patients who looked fat, with appropriate advice.

Oxford Prevention of Heart Attack and Stroke Project

Audit of general practice records indicated low levels of risk factor recording, so in 1982 a pilot project, the Oxford Prevention of Heart Attack and Stroke Project,[2] was initiated to assess the feasibility of implementing these recommendations, using practice nurses to identify patients at risk of cardiovascular disease. The results of this controlled trial showed that, compared with opportunistic ascertainment by GPs in consultations, a systematic approach by nurses, aided by a 'nurse facilitator', and recruiting patients attending the practice for other reasons, greatly improved recording of risk factors in practice records. Over a two and a half year period, recording of blood pressure was doubled, recording of smoking behaviour was quadrupled, and there was a five-fold increase in recording of weight in intervention practices compared with control practices.[3]

However, although the recruitment of patients was successful, there remained uncertainty about the extent to which this activity contributed to health. Follow-up of those found to be at high risk was incomplete,[4] there was a social class gradient in recruitment,[5] the adequacy of dietary advice in general practice was questionable,[6] and the effectiveness of smoking cessation advice by nurses in general practice seemed doubtful.[7]

The GP contract

In 1990, the government introduced a new GP contract which, among other things, effectively required GPs to provide health checks for newly registered patients, and periodically thereafter. By offering financial incentives to provide these health checks in health promotion clinics, the GP contract strongly encouraged nurse-conducted health checks. The contract has since been modified and health promotion clinic payments replaced by a banding system which does not discriminate between 'opportunistic' and 'clinic' activities (see Appendix 1.)

The OXCHECK Study

In the meantime, because of the uncertainties, planning for the OXCHECK (Oxford and Collaborators Health Check) Study began in 1987 and the trial to assess whether health checks by nurses are effective started in 1989.[8]

The OXCHECK Study was a randomised controlled trial. The study subjects comprised the entire 35-64 year old population of five group general practices in Luton and Dunstable in Bedfordshire. A total of

11,090 patients, an estimated 80% of the aggregate population in this age group in the practices, completed a detailed questionnaire covering lifestyle, history of cardiovascular disease, attitudes to health, and social and educational factors. All 11,090 were randomised at the outset to be invited for a health check in one of four 12-month periods between 1989 and 1993.

The health check included enquiry about relevant personal and family history and detailed information about diet, smoking, alcohol and physical activity. Examination included measurement of weight, height and blood pressure, according to protocols; a venous blood sample was taken for cholesterol measurement and for cotinine estimation to confirm smoking cessation. Initial health checks took about 45 minutes, follow-up examinations 10-20 minutes, and re-examinations about 30 minutes. Nurses were trained to counsel patients, with emphasis on eliciting patients' views and negotiating priorities. Dietary advice included use of a food frequency chart with a scoring system. Follow-up was by structured protocols for high blood pressure and hyper-lipidaemia and the intensity of follow-up was related to degree of risk. Priorities and targets were negotiated with patients in the light of overall risk.

The results of this intervention were the differences in risk factor levels in those returning for re-checks after a given interval compared with those coming for their initial check at that time. The mean levels of risk factors in the groups were compared and analysis was conducted both on an 'intention to treat' basis (ie including those who did not come for follow-up, as well as attenders, in the intervention group) and also on a 're-attenders only' basis. The former is the accepted, more conservative scientific analysis as it assumes that those not followed up remained unchanged; the latter will exaggerate benefits, as non-attenders would probably have been less compliant. The true result for the trial probably lies somewhere between the two.

One-year results
One-year follow-up results indicated substantial differences between intervention and control groups in reported diet and physical activity, smaller but significant differences in blood pressure and cholesterol levels, and no differences in smoking prevalence or smoking cessation, or in body mass index.[9] Mean total cholesterol was 2.3% lower and mean systolic and diastolic blood pressure 2.5% and 2.4% respectively lower in the intervention group compared with the control group.

When analysis was restricted only to those who came back for follow-up examination, the differences were 3.2%, 3.2% and 3.0% respectively.

This evidence indicated that, although health checks did work, their effect was modest. It was concluded that, nevertheless, the public health benefits of these reductions in cholesterol and blood pressure could be important, but this depended on the extent to which they might be sustained in the longer term. The lack of effect on smoking was disappointing but was consistent with the results of a previous trial of smoking cessation advice in health checks,[7] though at variance with the results of studies where smoking cessation intervention was not diluted by other health promotion messages.[10]

Three-year results

Three-year results, based on follow-up in 1992/93 of those receiving an initial health check in year 1 (1989/90) show that the effects were sustained.[11] Mean cholesterol was 3.0% lower, mean systolic and diastolic blood pressure 1.9% lower, and mean body mass index 1.4% lower in the intervention group, compared with controls. Frequency distribution curves of cholesterol levels showed greater benefit at the upper end of the distribution. Restricting the analysis only to those attending for follow-up showed that mean cholesterol level was 4.0% lower (5.2% in women and 2.6% in men), compared with controls. But again, there were no differences in smoking prevalence or smoking cessation.

These results provide firm evidence that the effects of health checks are sustained. There was no evidence that annual re-checks, after an initial health check, were more effective in modifying risk factors after three years than a single health check.[11] However, record audit showed that health checks generated follow-up visits, so the benefits of the intervention may be attributable to this as well as to the initial check.

Implications of the OXCHECK Study

Based on an overview of the effects of reduction of cholesterol and blood pressure on cardiovascular risk, it is estimated that the effect of widespread application of the intervention would be a reduction in long-term risk of myocardial infarction, attributable to the cholesterol lowering, of about 5% in men and 13% in women, and a further reduction of 7% in risk of myocardial infarction attributable to the blood pressure reduction.

The evidence from the OXCHECK Study is that nurse-conducted health checks work, to a limited degree. Their main effect was seen to be in dietary change and cholesterol reduction. However, there remain unanswered questions. Can these results be replicated, or perhaps improved, outside the research setting? Is the effort put into recruitment of patients (which involved up to three invitations) justified, or appropriate? What are the workload implications, and can the burden of work be sustained in the longer term? Is this a cost-effective intervention in public health terms? Are the psychological disbenefits outweighed by the gains? Or should primary care concentrate on secondary prevention in patients with established disease?

Dr Godfrey Fowler is an individual member of the National Heart Forum.

References

1 Royal College of General Practitioners. 1981. *Prevention of Arterial Disease in General Practice.* London: Royal College of General Practitioners.

2 Fullard E, Fowler G, Gray JAM. 1984. Facilitating prevention in primary care. *British Medical Journal;* 289: 1585-1587.

3 Fullard E, Fowler G, Gray JAM. 1987. Promoting prevention in primary care: controlled trial of low technology, low cost approach. *British Medical Journal;* 294: 1080-1082.

4 Mant D, McKinnley C, Fuller A, Randall A, Fullard E, Muir J. 1989. Three year follow-up of patients with raised blood pressure identified at health checks in general practice. *British Medical Journal;* 298: 1360-1362.

5 Waller D, Agass M, Mant D, Coulter A, Fuller A, Jones L. 1990. Health checks in general practice: another example of inverse care? *British Medical Journal;* 300: 1115-1118.

6 Frances J, Roche M, Mant D, Jones L, Fullard E. 1989. Would primary care workers give appropriate dietary advice after cholesterol screening? *British Medical Journal;* 296: 1620-1622.

7 Sanders D, Fowler G, Mant D, Jones L, Marzillier J. 1989. Randomised controlled trial of anti-smoking advice by nurses in primary care. *Journal of the Royal College of General Practitioners;* 39: 273-276.

8 Imperial Cancer Research Fund OXCHECK Study Group. 1991. Prevalence of risk factors for heart disease in OXCHECK trial: implications for screening in primary care. *British Medical Journal;* 302: 1057-1060.

9 Imperial Cancer Research Fund OXCHECK Study Group. 1994. Effectiveness of health checks conducted by nurses in primary care: results of the OXCHECK study after one year. *British Medical Journal;* 308: 308-312.

10 Imperial Cancer Research Fund General Practice Research Group. 1994. Randomised trial of nicotine patches in general practice: results at one year. *British Medical Journal;* 308: 1476-1477.

11 Imperial Cancer Research Fund OXCHECK Study Group. 1995. Effectiveness of health checks conducted by nurses in primary care: final results from the OXCHECK study. 1995. *British Medical Journal;* 310: 1099-1104.

Coronary heart disease prevention in primary care: two studies

The British Family Heart Study

Professor David Wood

Department of Clinical Epidemiology, National Heart and Lung Institute

The British Family Heart Study[1,2] was conceived in 1988 and, after a pilot study at Aldermoor Health Centre in Southampton in 1989, the main study was launched in 13 towns throughout Britain in 1990. The overall aim was to estimate the size of change in cardiovascular risk factors in men and women that could be achieved by a nurse-led cardiovascular screening and lifestyle intervention programme in families over one year. Specifically, the main objective was to measure the effect of one year's intervention on:

* total coronary risk score assessed with the Dundee risk score for three modifiable risk factors (cigarette smoking, blood pressure, and cholesterol concentration), and

* the prevalence of cigarette smoking and the distribution of weight, blood pressure, and random blood cholesterol and glucose concentrations in the population.

Design of the study

The design of this randomised controlled trial is summarised in Figure 1. In each of 13 towns, two selected practices were randomly allocated to the intervention or comparison arm of the trial. Families were identified through the male partner based on the practice list of men aged 40-59 years.

In the intervention practices, men and their families were approached by nurses telephoning the household. The initial screening interview for an adult couple lasted on average one and a half hours. This

Figure 1   **Design of the British Family Heart Study**

This figure shows the numbers of men and women seen at baseline and one year in the intervention group, and at one year in the internal and external comparison groups.

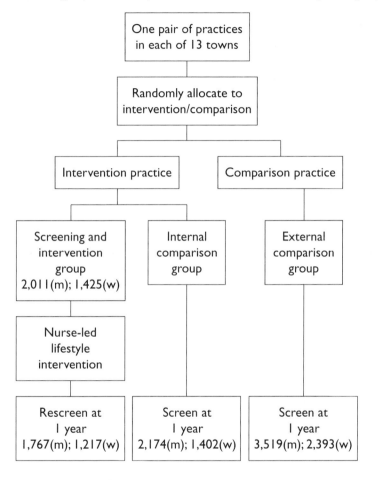

provided demographic, lifestyle and medical information as well as measurements of height and weight, blood pressure and random blood concentrations of total cholesterol and glucose. A coronary risk score was calculated, based on both modifiable and unmodifiable risk factors, and subjects were told which decile of risk distribution for coronary heart disease (CHD) they were in relative to other men (or women) of the same age. Those who reported a history of CHD, or chest pain on exercise, were automatically placed in the top decile of risk. The risk score was recorded in a booklet, *Your Passport to Health*, in which personally negotiated lifestyle changes in relation to smoking, weight, healthy eating, alcohol consumption and exercise could be documented.

The frequency of follow-up visits was determined by both the coronary risk score and individual risk factors. Adults (either partner) in the top quintile of the risk distribution, for example, were offered follow-up every two months, those in the fourth quintile every three months, and so on. People with individual high risk factors - current cigarette smokers and those with a body mass index >25 kg/m^2, diastolic blood pressure >90mmHg, cholesterol concentration >6.5mmol/l, or random glucose concentration >7.0mmol/l - were also invited to re-attend every month for up to three visits. If one or more of these individual risk factors was still high at the end of this period a referral to the GP was made.

Results

A total of 14,086 households were approached; 8,605 households were represented by one or more adult members, giving a crude household response rate of 61%. After adjustment of the denominator for 'ghosts' the true response rate was 73%. At one year, the re-attendance rate of men and women in the intervention group was 88% and 85% respectively. A total of 7,460 men and 5,012 women were studied in the intervention and comparison groups.

Dundee risk score
The Dundee risk score was approximately 16% lower at one year in the intervention group compared with either the external or internal comparison group (see Figure 2). The overall difference in coronary risk score was similar in men and women, but seemed to be rather more consistent across the 13 towns for men. The distribution of risk scores shows that the difference was greatest at the top (high-risk) end of the distribution. Of the observed 16% lower risk score in men (as compared with the external comparison group), 7% was attributed to blood pressure, 5% to smoking and 4% to cholesterol.

Cardiovascular risk factors
Individual differences in risk factors were similar in men and women, with both comparison groups giving consistent results. In the intervention group at one year:
- reported cigarette smoking among returners was lower by about 4%

Figure 2 **Mean differences in Dundee risk score, British Family Heart Study**

This figure shows the mean differences in Dundee risk score (intervention group minus external comparison group) with bars showing 95% confidence intervals for each of the 13 towns, and combined overall, for men and women separately.

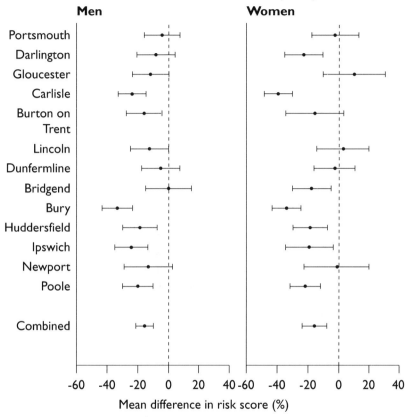

- systolic blood pressure was lower by an average of 7mmHg
- diastolic pressure was lower by 3mmHg
- weight was lower by an average of about 1kg, and
- cholesterol concentration was lower by an average of about 0.1mmol/l.

There was no discernible difference in median random blood glucose concentration.

The differences in the distribution of systolic blood pressure and serum cholesterol concentration showed a consistent tendency for greater changes at the top of the distribution than at the bottom. The proportions of subjects with high blood pressure (diastolic blood pressure >100mmHg), high cholesterol concentration (>8.0mmol/l), or high body mass index (>30 kg/m²) were lower in the intervention group than the comparison group but there was no discernible difference in the proportions with high random blood glucose concentrations (>10.0mmol/l).

The numbers of men and women referred to their GPs by the nurses with very high or sustained high individual risk factor values, expressed as a proportion of the total population screened, were respectively:
- blood pressure (diastolic > 90mmHg): 2% and 1%
- cholesterol (> 6.5mmol/l): 5% and 5%
- glucose concentration (> 7mmol/l): 3% and 1%.
In the whole population there was no reported difference between the intervention and comparison groups in the proportions of patients taking drugs to lower blood pressure or cholesterol concentrations or for diabetes. The proportions of patients at one year with reported CHD were similar in intervention and comparison groups.

Non-returners
The intervention group necessarily comprised those who were recruited to the study one year before and who also returned at one year, while for the comparison group the one-year appointment represented their first screening visit. There was a much greater prevalence of cigarette smoking among those who did not return compared to those who did. Weight was on average slightly higher among the non-returners, but no other major risk factors showed clear differences. There was, however, generally a slightly higher prevalence of CHD and diagnosed diabetes, reported high blood pressure, and high blood cholesterol concentration among those who returned compared with those who did not.

Discussion

In this national trial of nurse-led cardiovascular screening and lifestyle intervention in general practice, the overall Dundee risk score was 16% lower after intervention. A lower blood pressure accounted for almost half of the observed lower risk, smoking for one-third and cholesterol concentration for about a quarter. The true difference in coronary risk, however, is actually less for two reasons. Firstly, differences in smoking are considerably smaller when the smoking habits of those who did not return at one year are taken into account. Secondly, lower blood pressure is likely to be partly due to measurement acclimatisation in the intervention group.

The lower smoking prevalence observed in the intervention group is biased by two factors. Firstly, a proportion of those recruited at baseline did not return at one year (12% of men and 15% of women), and the prevalence of smoking at baseline among these non-returners was more than twice as high in both men and women compared to those who did return. Secondly, those returning in the intervention group at one year may also have under-reported cigarette smoking. If it is assumed that the participants seen at baseline who did not return at one year had not altered their smoking habit, and among the reported ex-cigarette smokers those with a breath carbon monoxide concentration of over 10ppm were in fact still smoking cigarettes, the observed reduction in the crude proportion of cigarette smokers of 3.9% in men (compared with the internal comparison group) should be adjusted to 1%, and for women 3.8% should be adjusted to 0.7%. Thus the difference in prevalence of smoking between returners and non-returners clearly considerably weakens the evidence for a crude reduction in cigarette smoking in the intervention group.

The observed lower blood pressure may be partly due to the acclimatisation or habituation effect with repeated measurements over time. It is difficult to assess the extent to which the reduction in blood pressure associated with intervention in this study could be due to such acclimatisation. Using directly comparable data in a population with repeated blood pressure measurements, there is on average a reduction of 3.5mmHg systolic and 1.5mmHg diastolic in men, and almost identical results in women. These data suggest that acclimatisation may therefore explain about half the reduction in blood pressure observed in this study.

So, with no change in cigarette smoking taken together with a reduction of 1.5mmHg in diastolic blood pressure (half that observed), and a reduction of 0.1mmol/l in blood cholesterol, the long-term proportionate reduction in CHD risk, assuming that these changes in risk factors are maintained long term, is estimated to be about 12%. This risk reduction was achieved by changes in lifestyle as there was no difference at one year in the use of drugs to lower blood pressure and cholesterol concentration between the intervention and comparison groups. A risk reduction of 12% in men aged 40-59 participating in a national programme could potentially prevent 788 myocardial infarctions and 853 deaths from CHD each year in the UK, which is about 8% of all such events in British men of this age.

Summary

This large national trial demonstrated that an intensive cardiovascular screening and intervention in general practice lowered blood pressure and blood cholesterol concentration at one year in the intervention group. If these small reductions could be sustained in the long term they will correspond to a 12% lower risk of CHD events in 73% of the population. As this lower risk was achieved with a family-based programme led by nurses trained in learner-centred techniques, and with intensive follow-up in relation to overall CHD risk, as well as individual risk factors, the government-sponsored health promotion clinic sessions, with no financial commitment to follow-up, would probably have achieved considerably less and possibly no change at all. Whether the new health promotion package for general practice, which encourages a more opportunistic approach to screening the population reflecting the reiterative contact between patients and the primary care team, will achieve useful reductions in risk must remain in considerable doubt and cannot be justified in its present form from the results of the British Family Heart Study.

Other options might include focusing limited primary care resources on high-risk patients - for example, those with hypertension, hyperlipidaemia, diabetes and established CHD. Whatever new approaches are advocated, this trial emphasises the need for, and shows the feasibility of, rigorous scientific evaluation to measure the impact of such strategies in the future. Primary care alone cannot provide a population approach to reducing cardiovascular risk, and the government, in aiming to reduce the prevalence of risk factors, will also need to put in place more effective public health policies on tobacco control and healthy eating.

Professor David Wood represents the British Cardiac Society on the National Heart Forum.

References

1   Wood DA, Kinmonth AL, Pyke SDM, Thompson SG on behalf of the Family Heart Study Group. 1994. A randomised controlled trial evaluating cardiovascular screening and intervention in general practice: principal results of the British Family Heart Study. *British Medical Journal*; 308: 313-320.

2   Wood DA, Kinmonth AL, Davies G, Yarwood J, Thompson SG, Pyke SDM, Kok Y, Cramb R, Guen CL on behalf of the British Family Heart Study Group. 1994. Cardiovascular risk factors in the Family Heart Study. A national randomised controlled trial evaluating cardiovascular screening and interventions in British general practice. *British Journal of General Practice*; 44: 62-67.

Chapter 3

Interventions in primary care

A population approach to interventions in primary care: assessing the evidence

Professor Klim McPherson

Professor of Public Health Epidemiology, Department of Public Health and Policy, London School of Hygiene and Tropical Medicine

Coronary heart disease (CHD) has a multifactorial aetiology, appears to be eminently preventable, and is common in developed societies. What is the evidence for encouraging uni- or multifactorial interventions among populations in primary care? Broadly the answer is that the evidence, particularly when balanced with the putative costs, seems not very strong. The next question is 'How does this evidence bear on the policy question concerning appropriate investment in health gain, as compared with other policies?'

But that bald statement about weak evidence has to be understood in the context of what constitutes, or could possibly constitute, strong evidence. In the context in which medical interventions are (or should be) evaluated, a series of excellent prospective randomised controlled trials would be required, in which population interventions have fairly consistently been associated with an important reduction in CHD incidence or death compared with controls.

That is clearly not now the case, as the critics of health promotion are quick to point out.[1] Secondary prevention trials of dietary interventions typically produce a few percentage points of cholesterol reduction.[2] Intensive dietary interventions among a few well motivated subjects can produce more dramatic reductions in serum cholesterol levels.[3] Appropriate interventions can reduce blood pressure and hence risk.

Smoking cessation in the health care context is also well studied and known to be effective in specific contexts.[4]

So why are population interventions in primary care not being widely advocated and funded? The answer is that proper randomised intervention trials do not show conclusive evidence for much benefit for a population approach. Some therefore favour an opportunistic intervention[5] and others worry, quite reasonably, about cost-effectiveness ratios.

In such an ambience there should be appropriate cynicism about the possibility of benefit but at the same time care should be taken not to throw the baby out with the bath water, until more is known about what is effective and what is not, and what is truly cost-effective and what is not. Before drawing any conclusions three aspects should be emphasised in this brief review of the evidence:

- What is conclusive evidence in the circumstances?
- What are the problems with the current evidence?
- What do we still need to find out - that is knowable?

What is conclusive evidence?

Firstly, the evidence favouring a multifactorial, as opposed to a unifactorial, and a population, as opposed to a high-risk, approach is, in principle, overwhelming. There is no doubt that the vast majority of premature cardiovascular events in our society occur among people who have relatively low levels of a few risk factors only.[6] The events which occur among people with high designated levels of acknowledged risk factors are a minority of all events. The questions surround the effectiveness and appropriateness of multifactorial interventions among such populations. However, a relatively small attributable effect on some risk factors among populations would be important.

Secondly, there is convincing evidence, from a multitude of sources, that the primary care team is currently the dominant, and deemed to be the most reliable, source of medical information for populations in the UK.[7] There are problems to do with comprehension and credibility trends that can give rise to no complacency. However, a survey has shown doctors to be still high in terms of their role in moral guidance.

The problem has to do with the effectiveness of any intervention designed to reduce the cardiac risk among populations in primary care. Successfully attributing effectiveness to interventions is generally complicated. In contrast to prevention policies, evaluating therapeutic treatments is systematically easier. This is because they are specific to the patient and his or her disease, and always administered by enthusiasts for the therapeutic role. They are often based on finely tuned and validated biological knowledge. They can be a consequence of sophisticated laboratory information, tailored often to a particular organ system. Finding the evidence for effectiveness often relies on observing quite large effects and reliably measured outcomes on well defined, often small, (randomised) groups of ill people, consequently for a relatively short time.[8]

This is the paradigm through which evidence is now gathered and by which its conclusiveness and relevance are judged. It might though require some slight adjustment for the interpretation of evaluations of *preventive* interventions for the following five reasons.

1   Health promotion interventions are not specific, often poorly measured, sometimes based on poorly understood, complex psychological and sociological phenomenon and are commonly contaminated with many external influences on free healthy populations. These populations are large, very heterogeneous and often poorly defined, and observing the relevant final hard outcomes has to be delayed, among fit individuals, often for decades.

Finding the evidence for the effectiveness for some things will therefore be naturally easier than for others. It should be clear that finding the evidence for the effectiveness of health promotion will be systematically much more difficult than finding similar relative sizes of effects of treatments. Thus the evidence about outcomes will have a different role in influencing policy because of the intrinsic differences in the ability to reliably find it.

Some argue that, notwithstanding the above considerations, the implementation of health promotion strategies should, for ethical reasons, have to await *conclusive* evidence of effectiveness.[9] If this is accepted policy, much potential preventive medicine cannot be taken as a serious option at all, apart from well established, often biologically specific, vaccinations and immunisations. The implications of this apparent double jeopardy, particularly associated with behavioural interventions, have to be recognised fully by all concerned. If that is the real reason for disparaging such interventions in primary care, and seemingly unimpressive trial results are used as justification, then the argument is dishonest.

In this case of establishing the attributable effect of multifactorial interventions, almost everything is duly attenuated by the complicated processes involved in the mechanisms required to make such programmes work. The follow-up is as yet short. The controls are not strictly comparable for fear of contamination, and yet contamination is not necessarily avoided. The interventions may not themselves be optimal, administered by people whose training and vocation may not be in disease prevention or in health promotion. Furthermore the populations included are of relatively low risk anyway.[10, 11]

2 Useful models for the effectiveness of interventions designed to alter behaviour, such as Prochaska's stages of change model,[12] tell us that the response to health messages depends on the particular stages of change that subjects may be in. The OXCHECK Study and the British Family Heart Study do not have information about where the subjects are with respect to their individual stages and each relevant behaviour change. Thus the response to an intervention may well be a function of some exogenous factor which itself is strongly determined by social and psychological factors and for which there may be strong systematic temporal, geographic, social and other correlates and determinants.

However, biology is normally taken to be more stable than that, which is why extrapolation from one or two trials may then be more secure. In the circumstances now under consideration, however, such extrapolation may simply be premature and irresponsible. If most of the subjects were in a precontemplative stage with respect to their behaviour concerning a key risk factor, then an extremely modest effect would be predicted. However, that would not necessarily predict the results of another trial among people more commonly in a contemplative or preparation stage. And if the intervention simply shifts people through stages, then the outcome measures used are inappropriate.

3 Another phenomenon, often discussed in the evaluation of surgical treatments, is the learning curve. In this case not only might populations become more receptive but the primary care team might become much more effective and potent. It seems clear that the business of learning how to provide, in an acceptable, effective and efficient way, health information that is useful to patients is in its infancy.[13] The task is certainly difficult, since it is so complex, and the evidence on its effectiveness is currently unimpressive. Moreover, talking to primary care professionals gives rise to a strong impression that an important proportion simply do not regard disease prevention and health promotion as their vocation. This must be an important but expected observation, since they were trained to treat illness.

4 The above arguments suggest that the major hypothesis has yet to be properly tested. There is another difference for policy implementation between preventive and therapeutic interventions. Therapeutic interventions are specific and individual. They can be developed, improved and implemented and, once consolidated, can be sensitively tested. With a preventive policy the intervention has to be developed and defined years before it is implemented and then it takes a long time for the effect to happen. This is another disadvantage for demonstrating effectiveness. The bath water is still too easily confused with the baby, simply because the opportunities for the baby to grow and mature are massively laborious and commonly underestimated.

5 Within the paradigm of clinical testing the effect is a particular direct effect of the intervention among the subjects randomised. In prevention, the behavioural manifestations of any attributable effect may not be as straightforward but can still be ultimately beneficial.

A preventive intervention could also act in a more dispersed manner by influencing others and thus contaminating or diluting the measurement of intervention effect. There is much evidence for a significant effect of control as a consequence of empowerment having very indirect effects on CHD which may not be measured by established risk factors.[14] There is also much evidence for an intervention affecting the health behaviour of controls in a beneficial manner.[15] These effects, some of which may be potent, may be attributable to the intervention, but will not be acknowledged as such in the published results.

Thus the most rigorous method of evaluation usually relies on tight biological processes and well titrated interventions. It also relies on precise measurement and minimal misclassification and does best when treatments are administered uniformly by enthusiasts. Often a relatively homogeneous biological system is expected, not greatly moderated by external factors. Moreover the outcomes by which effectiveness is to be compared are relevant and specific and exclusive to the patient.

In the circumstances of a complex preventive intervention, none of these features apply to anything like the same extent and hence it seems wrong to interpret the results of these two trials as if they did. The implications need to be given serious consideration. These are that a modest effect in these two trials possibly gives rise to illegitimate despair.

The major differences between evaluating a preventive intervention compared with a therapeutic intervention are summarised in Table 1.

Each of these intrinsic factors tends to mean that a given proportional effect of a given kind of study is rendered more difficult to detect in prevention. Thus, seemingly equivocal evidence need not sensibly lead to the same conclusions in either situation.

Table I   Evaluating interventions in health

Preventive	Therapeutic
behavioural	biological
long-term effects	short-term effects
rare endpoints	common endpoints
'soft' endpoints	'hard' endpoints
largely public policy	largely individual decisions
initiated/imposed	demand-led
well 'clients'	ill 'clients'
small proportion benefit	large proportion benefit
applicable to groups	applicable to individuals

What are the problems with the current evidence?

The current evidence suggests modest effects attributed to the OXCHECK Study and British Family Heart Study interventions so far. But one would have expected little else. A massive community intervention in Finland[16] gave rise to a change in risk status among men and women in the first year which is entirely similar to the results of the two UK studies, both with respect to aggregate findings and heterogeneity of apparent response. In Finland the ultimate effect was a reduction in risk factors both predicting and observing a 40% reduction in mortality after 20 years. Some risk factors were apparently reduced in one gender only in the first year and others were unexpectedly disappointing. But chance has peculiar manifestations. That is why having only a few trials is such a disadvantage because one is too tempted to take each individual measured outcome difference as the truth, because there is such a paucity of other experimental data.

In the OXCHECK Study and the British Family Heart Study the intervention was a single entity. Given the difficulties mentioned above, it is not clear why the conclusion should be that such interventions are not sufficiently effective. They may not be, but these data certainly do not go very far towards proving it. It seems more likely that these interventions are the beginning, and possibly only one component, of something very important in a sensible programme to reduce unwanted premature mortality.

These trials were looking for a small attributable effect on a large number, which translates into a small average change. They have found it, against all the odds. Almost everything intrinsic to the experimental set-up might have conspired towards such an effect not being found. Since essentially it was found, it seems most likely therefore that the ultimate effect of well refined, well motivated specific interventions on populations who have some enthusiasm for change might work much better.

A cool interpretation of the current evidence suggests that it is much what would have been expected by those who believe that primary prevention through multifactorial interventions will work among populations with moderate levels of a few risk factors. Clearly the potency of some of the interventions could be improved upon, particularly smoking in the OXCHECK Study and possibly cholesterol in the British Family Heart Study. But these improvements must be worked on in all health promotion interventions and titrated appropriately to the empowered citizens.

A summary of the results of the OXCHECK Study and British Family Heart Study, and of the interpolated first year results of the community intervention project in North Karelia, Finland, is given in Table 2. The North Karelia project went on to produce dramatic public health effects. To ignore the evidence from the OXCHECK Study and the British Family Heart Study is clearly to run the serious risk of missing an important role attributable to primary care in public health.

Table 2 **Most conservative aggregate effects in three studies**

	On risk factors at 1 year (%)		
	OXCHECK Study	British Family Heart Study	North Karelia project, Finland
Cholesterol	2.2	2.2	0.9
Blood pressure			
Systolic	2.5	5.8	
Diastolic	2.3	3.4	1.1
BMI/Weight	0.6	1.5	
Smoking prevention	-0.5	3.6	1.0

What do we still need to find out - that is knowable?

The interesting part of this question involves the poorly explored extent to which the risk levels of a community are merely the sum of the risk levels of each individual or whether the nature, practices and culture of the community itself also have effects on these risk levels. It also involves the extent to which the business of changing risk levels for the better is more efficiently achieved through community participation than through individual members of that community.[17]

The extent to which the role of the primary care team affects, and is affected by, these matters also needs to be carefully explored. The measured role of primary care interventions on the risk levels of individuals among randomly selected groups has already been discussed. But it is important to know how these effects are moderated by intrinsic risks in a community and how they relate to other aspects of public health policy such as a tobacco advertising ban and a national nutrition policy. The question is 'To what extent do multifactorial interventions in primary care simply move populations through relevant stages of change?' If that is the hypothesis then the outcomes should not be measured levels of risk factors.

Another area which deserved more investigation is the possible augmentation of an effect using interactive video techniques to provide specific information about risk. The idea is that information which is specific to the person participating, both with respect to their own risk factors and with respect to the manner in which risk is presented, is more acceptable and effective. Such facilities could give the best estimate of the effect of any changes which the participant was willing to postulate on life chances. It would be quite easy to manufacture such software. The use of interactive video discs for informing patients about their symptoms and their treatment is being investigated. The results are interesting because they demonstrate that patients react in very disparate but, in their view, entirely rational ways and that they tend not to respond in the manner predicted. They particularly do not necessarily respond in the manner their medical adviser would recommend.

In the end of course an intervention policy designed to benefit the health of the public must be justified by its effectiveness, its acceptability and its cost. A study has shown quite attractive cost-effectiveness ratios for some so-called opportunistic strategies among populations.[18] This work uses the OXCHECK attributable effects on risk as its basis. The relationship these factors have with stages of change and risk in the short term, and morbidity in the long term, are the crucial determinants of appropriate public health policy.

In some instances concentrating on high-risk individuals will obviously be better than a general non-specific policy. In terms of acceptability it is often stigmatising, and therefore alienating, to have a policy directed at particular individuals in a community characterised in a particular (high-risk) way. The strong tradition in medicine is of course to identify sick individuals and treat them as if divorced from the community from which they come. In prevention it is quite possible that a generalised message made specific to individuals is quite as potent and as valid, and possibly much more effective, than one concentrating on particular high-risk individuals. That this is not the case remains totally unproven.

Conclusion

In the 1970s a trial undertaken in primary care of a multifactorial screening intervention demonstrated no reduction in cardiovascular risk,[19] and this is possibly the basis of our cynicism. However, the present evidence should not be the cause of continued despair. It should be an encouragement to experiment and to study further in order to refine the interventions.

Cervical screening in general practice is now well established and fairly clearly beneficial, but the cost for the programme of each life saved is calculated as £100,000.[20] Nobody has ever demonstrated effectiveness in clinical trials. For years the service was inefficiently provided and probably ineffective.[21] But the process has hopefully led eventually to greater knowledge and a better service.

It seems clear that a proper interpretation of the evidence from the OXCHECK Study and the British Family Heart Study suggests a continued evolution of the role of primary care in primary prevention, in a manner which acknowledges all the evidence and enables efficient improvement in the approach.[22]

Professor Klim McPherson is an individual member of the National Heart Forum.

References

1   Le Fanu J. 1994. *Preventionitis. The Exaggerated Claims of Health Promotion*. London: The Social Affairs Unit.

2   Multiple Risk Factor Intervention Trial Research Group. 1982. Multiple risk factor intervention trial: risk factor changes and mortality results. *Journal of the American Medical Association*; 248: 1465-1477.

3   Burr M. 1994. Clinical trials of altering dietary fat intake. *Journal of Cardiovascular Risk*; 1; 1: 38-43.

4   Sanders D. 1992. *Smoking Cessation Interventions: Is Patient Education Effective?* London: Health Promotion Sciences Unit, PHP Departmental Publication No. 6.

5   Stott N. 1994. Screening for cardiovascular risk in general practice; blanket health promotion is a waste of resources. *British Medical Journal*; 308: 285-286.

6   Rose G. 1992. *The Strategy of Preventive Medicine*. Oxford: Oxford University Press.

7   Griffin J. 1994. *Health Information and the Consumer*. OHE Briefing.

8   McPherson K. 1994. Health promotion under fire. *Lancet*; 344: 890-891.

9   McCormick J. 1994. Health promotion: the ethical dimension. *Lancet*; 344: 390-391.

10   Imperial Cancer Research Fund OXCHECK Study Group. 1994. Effectiveness of health checks conducted by nurses in primary care. Results of the OXCHECK Study after one year. *British Medical Journal*; 308: 308-312.

11   Family Heart Study Group. 1994. Randomised controlled trial evaluating cardio-vascular screening and intervention in general practice: principal results of the British Family Heart Study. *British Medical Journal*; 308: 313-320.

12   Prochaska JO, DiClemente C, Norcross JC. 1992. In search of how people change. *American Psychologist*; 47: 1102-1114.

13   Donati Pierpaolo. The need for new social policy perspectives in health-behaviour research. In: Anderson R et al (eds). 1988. *Health Behaviour Research and Health Promotion*. Oxford: Oxford University Press.

14   McPherson K. 1994. The Cochrane lecture. The best and the enemy of the good: randomised controlled trials, uncertainty, and assessing the role of patient choice in medical decision making. *Journal of Epidemiology and Community Health*; 48: 6-15.

15   WHO European Collaborative Group. 1986. European collaborative trial of multifac-torial prevention of coronary heart disease: Final report on the 6 year results. *Lancet*; (ii): 869-872.

16   Viatiainen E, Puska P, Pekkanen J et al. 1994. Changes in risk factors explain changes in mortality from ischaemic heart disease in Finland. *British Medical Journal*; 309: 23-27.

17   Blackburn H. 1992. Community programmes in coronary heart disease prevention and health promotion: changing community behaviour. In: Marmot M, Elliot P (eds). 1992. *Coronary Heart Disease Epidemiology*. Oxford: Oxford University Press.

18   Field K, Thorogood M, Silagy C, Normand C, O'Neill C, Muir J. 1995. Strategies for reducing coronary risk factors in primary care: which is most effective? *British Medical Journal*; 310: 1109-1112.

19   The South East London Screening Group. 1977. A controlled trial of multiphasic screening in middle-age; the results of the South East London screening study. *International Journal of Epidemiology*; 6: 357-363.

20   First five years of the NHS cervical screening programme. National coordinating network 1994. Reported in *Independent*: 12th October 1994.

21   Raffle AE, Alden B, Mackenzie EFD. 1995. Detection rates for abnormal cervical smears: what are we screening for? *Lancet*; 345: 1469-1473.

22   Silagy C, Mant D, Carpenter L, Muir J, Neil A. 1994. Modelling different strategies to prevent coronary heart disease in primary care. *Journal of Clinical Epidemiology*; 47: 993-1001.

Health-related behaviour change

Professor Marie Johnston

Department of Psychology, University of St Andrews

Models of behaviour change

Models of behaviour change have been very influential in guiding research and practice by behavioural and social scientists working in health-related areas, but have not necessarily impinged on the practice of other professions in the field. Simple models such as that illustrated in Figure 1 have clearly been demonstrated to be inadequate to describe the process. However, they may still be the implicit models when assumptions are unstated, with the result that naive attempts may be made to change behaviour by changing information and attitudes.

Figure 1   Simple model of behaviour change

Models such as this have clearly been demonstrated to be inadequate.

There have been three main scientifically based approaches to behaviour change: behavioural methodologies, social cognition models, and stages of change models.

Behavioural methodologies

The behavioural and cognitive-behavioural therapies were derived originally from the treatment of psychological problems. These methods attempted to predict and control behaviour based on assessment and manipulation of antecedents and consequences and were based on the theoretical work of Skinner and Pavlov earlier this century.

Methods such as rewards, prompts, goal-setting, and self-monitoring[1] have been found to be effective in achieving desired behaviour change, including health-related behaviour, and have been used in a controlled trial of methods of giving feedback following worksite screening for behavioural risk factors.[2, 3]

While these methods have been well established and widely used by psychologists since the 1970s, their use has not permeated the medical literature relevant to health-related behaviour change. One can speculate about the reasons for this. Is it due to the failure of psychologists to publish their work in the medical literature? Or is it due to the limited education of doctors in psychology? However, of more relevance here is that health-related behaviour change may be implemented without awareness of such methods, and extremely costly clinical trials may be undertaken using interventions which have already been shown to be ineffective. Indeed, the reports of such trials may even omit to give a full description of the methods used with the result that methods could not be replicated if found to be effective and could not be discarded if found to be ineffective. An illustration of a more explicit description of methods is given by Perry et al,[4] of interventions used in the Minnesota Heart Health Programme.

These methods represent a very effective technology but there is no very satisfactory explanation of why they are effective. By contrast, social cognition models attempt to offer a better theoretical explanation of behaviour.

Social cognition models
Social cognition models deal with the thoughts and beliefs that people have about objects or events occurring in social situations. Two main models are applied in health-related behaviour research: the Health Belief Model and the Theory of Reasoned Action/Planned Behaviour. Other theoretical frameworks include Protection Motivation Theory,[5, 6] Social Learning/Cognitive Theory,[7] Attribution Theory,[8] and the Health Action Process.[9]

The Health Belief Model
The Health Belief Model[10] has performed an important function in research on health-related behaviour as it has encouraged researchers to adhere to an explicit model of the process rather than using intuitive, unshared models. First proposed in the 1960s, the Health Belief Model (see Figure 2) attempted to bring together what was known about the

situational and attitudinal factors involved in taking action relevant to health, such as engaging in dental care, attending for health checks, or giving up smoking. The main components are the perceived health threat, the expected benefits of and barriers to the proposed behaviours, and cues to action. Social, personal and demographic factors are also postulated to influence the process and more recently, health motivation and beliefs in self-efficacy (competence to enact the behaviour) have been included. The model has been used in understanding and predicting all sorts of health-related behaviours.[11, 12]

Figure 2 **Health Belief Model**

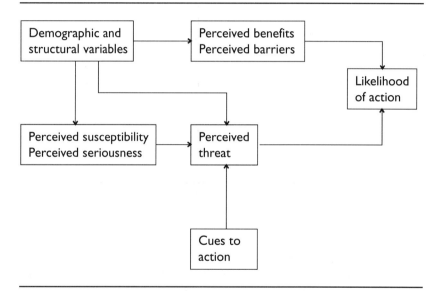

Source: See reference 10.

The main problems with the Health Belief Model are:

- The contents of the model
- The model assumes a rational decision-making process, when many behaviours that influence health may be habitual or influenced by social or emotional, rather than rational processes.
- It over-estimates the role of threat compared with empirical evidence on the topic.
- Cues to action are seen to influence perceived threat, but should more appropriately have a direct effect on the likelihood of preventive action.

- It has a limited and poorly specified role for the influence of other people.

• How it has been used
- Several versions of the Health Belief Model exist in different publications.
- When the model has been updated, this has seemed only to add complexity rather than to provide a more coherent model.
- There is no agreement on how to measure the main variables and so different studies may measure different constructs even when describing them by the same name.
- Measures used frequently lack evidence of reliability and validity.
- Frequently only single components rather than the full model are assessed, or there is incomplete statistical testing, using univariate rather than multivariate analyses and ignoring the proposed relationships between components of the model. For example, it is not clear what the model would predict if perceived susceptibility were high but there were no data on perceived severity.

• Predictive value
- The model typically explains only a small amount of variance in behaviour.

• Lack of integration with other theories of behaviour
- There is no *a priori* reason to expect health-related behaviour to follow different rules from other behaviour and one might therefore expect a general model of behaviour to be applicable.

Some, but not all of these criticisms apply also to the Theory of Reasoned Action/Planned Behaviour.

The Theory of Reasoned Action/Planned Behaviour
The Theory of Reasoned Action[13, 14] has undoubtedly been the most influential model of attitudes and behaviour. It proposes that behaviour is determined by behavioural intentions which are in turn determined by a combination of attitudes and social norms. Attitudes are a multiplicative function of beliefs about the likely outcomes of a specified behaviour and the value attached to these outcomes. Social norms are a multiplicative function of our beliefs about what other people would want us to do and our motivation to comply with their wishes. The authors proposed that social and environmental factors operate via the components of the model.

The main advances introduced by this model were:

- the influence of other people via social norms
- the focus on beliefs and attitudes toward the specific behaviour under study, and
- the mediating effect of behavioural intentions.

Since the development of the Theory of Reasoned Action, only one modification has been made: the addition of perceived behavioural control (a concept similar to self-efficacy) to produce what is now known as the Theory of Planned Behaviour[15] (see Figure 3). While this model still has some of the problems of the Health Belief Model, its components and methods of assessing them are more clearly specified. There is still some concern about how much variance the model predicts, with estimates typically varying between 20% and 40%, but perhaps this should be seen as a good start rather than a reason for abandoning it.

Figure 3   **Theory of Planned Behaviour**

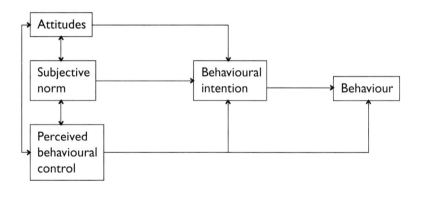

Source: See reference 15.

Because the model can be used to investigate any form of behaviour, it can be applied to behaviour relevant to health without assuming that the behaviour is influenced by health considerations. For example, use of condoms can readily be considered within this model as a social/interpersonal relationship behaviour rather than as a health-related behaviour. Uses of the model have been reviewed by Sheppard et al.[16]

Stages of change models

It has been argued that the processes involved in engaging in health-related behaviour and the explanatory variables are different at different stages or levels. This is an extremely important point for behavioural risk reduction programmes as it suggests that:
- models will have limited power to predict behaviour unless they take account of individual stages
- any population will contain individuals at different stages, and
- the interventions needed to change behaviour will be different for those at different stages.

Such assumptions are incorporated in the behaviour change methods which require individual analysis of current behaviour, its antecedents and consequences, but are not incorporated in the social cognition models. Models such as the Health Belief Model and Theory of Reasoned Action/Theory of Planned Behaviour propose that the processes involved in engaging in health-related behaviour are the same regardless of the current stage of beliefs of the individual.

The best known model, the Transtheoretical Model of Behaviour Change[17, 18] proposes that there are six stages in behaviour change:
- *precontemplation* - not intending to make changes
- *contemplation* - considering a change
- *preparation* - making small changes
- *action* - actively engaging in new behaviour
- *maintenance* - sustaining change over time
- *relapse* - relapsing back to an earlier stage.

The authors also proposed that the differences between stages were mediated by decisional-balance - the balance between the pros and cons of undertaking the change. Their studies of smoking and other studies of exercise engagement[19, 20] show the operation of decisional balance; pros only exceed cons at the stage of preparation.

An alternative but similar approach is Weinstein's Precaution Adoption Process.[21, 22] This model differs from the Transtheoretical Model of Behaviour Change in elaborating stages when the individual has not thought about making changes.

Current issues and developments

The three approaches presented function as separate literatures, but progress might come from attempting to reconcile the social-cognitive, behavioural and stages of change perspectives on behaviour change. Social cognition models might contribute fuller understanding to processes such as goal-setting, for example by clarifying the role of 'implementation intentions' in facilitating recall.[23, 24] Similarly, a more detailed study of the demonstrated effective behavioural interventions might define the processes requiring greater theoretical understanding. Further, Weinstein[21] has proposed that the three approaches can be brought together by suggesting that the critical behavioural and social-cognitive processes will depend on the individual's stage.

The behaviour of health professionals

The behaviour of health professionals may play a significant part in determining risk behaviour change. Like other human beings, their behaviours are likely to be influenced by their attitudes, social norms, behavioural intentions, self-efficacy beliefs, etc.[25] Patients may not be given advice on behavioural risk factor reduction because doctors may believe that changing the behaviour will not affect the risk factor (attitudes toward the behaviour), or because they believe they are incapable of giving appropriate dietary advice (self-efficacy concerning the behaviour), as found in a study of cholesterol screening.[26] Another study found that GPs' attitudes predicted rates of uptake of mammography in their patients.[27] The same study also points to the importance of rewards for the behaviour by noting the increased rates of screening following its inclusion in GP contracts, again indicating the importance of the behaviour of health professionals as well as patients.

The style of communication may limit effectiveness. Ley's Cognitive Hypothesis[28] summarises a large body of evidence in this field and proposes that patient satisfaction with medical communications can play a significant part in determining adherence to medical communications; satisfaction is influenced in turn by understanding and recall of information given. The method of informing can have undesirable side-effects. For example one study found that one message achieved both risk factor (high blood pressure) reduction and anxiety control, while the alternative message achieved risk factor reduction, but with high anxiety levels.[29] Previous research has pointed to the increased persuasiveness of medical figures in white coats, and such factors might influence the effectiveness of behaviour change advice.

Communication of research findings

Important behavioural processes come into play not only in the behaviour of patients and health professionals, but also in the behaviour of the researchers, particularly at the stage of interpreting results. In the editorial and letters following the British Family Heart Study[30] and the OXCHECK Study[31] comments ranged from "a waste of resources" to "a cause for celebration",[32] demonstrating the potential for different evaluations of the same findings. This highlights two problems: first the need to specify in advance what constitutes a 'finding of significance' and second, the possibility that interpretations of research findings display bias.

Numerous *post-hoc* criteria were applied to the interpretation of the results. Both studies interpreted the observed blood pressure effects as no greater than might be attributed to spurious effects of repeated measurement, even though the trials were designed to have the power to detect such effects. Perhaps in future trials, the size of finding which would satisfy the criteria for a 'finding of significance', rather than a 'significant finding', should be estimated in advance so that the debate about these matters which have an inevitable degree of arbitrariness can be conducted before the data become available.

The second point concerns the uni-directional and possibly biased nature of the *post hoc* argument. Ensuring that no insignificant finding is wrongly interpreted as significant is justified as costs incurred in implementing these programmes might be wasted and the scientific and medical communities misled by inaccurate use of data. But what of the possibility that a significant opportunity to reduce population morbidity and mortality by a small amount might be rejected? All of the *post hoc* arguments in the discussion of the results served to diminish rather than enhance the results. Counter-arguments were not aired. Counter-arguments might have included, for example, that contami-nation effects would serve to reduce intervention-control group differ-ence, that underlying population changes in risk factors might mask differences due to the interventions, that the interventions were directed towards individuals who had to date resisted the effects of other persuasive messages relevant to lifestyle, or that the interventions had not been designed and executed by specialists in behavioural change.

Such a bias might arise for a number of reasons. Firstly, current presentation as a good scientist may require more avoidance of falsely finding benefit than of failing to find true benefit. Secondly, it may be important to avoid finding support for new procedures at a time of financial stringency in the health services. The argument in the British Family Heart Study that a typical practice would require at least four full-time nurses was based on the arbitrary, and surely unnecessary, assumption that the total population should be screened in 18 months, thus adding an unusual bias to the argument. Thirdly, it may be 'acceptable' to criticise the effectiveness of nurses (see comment in reference 33). Fourthly, interventions involving behavioural rather than pharmacological implementation may have to satisfy higher or different standards of evidence; it has been suggested in an entirely different domain that if the benefits accruing from psychological preparation of patients for surgery[34] had been achieved by pharmacological means, then such preparation would become mandatory. Fifthly, the bias may have occurred because the results were poorer than expected, with the result that the authors were particularly critical of their findings.

Conclusions

Research in health-related behaviour frequently neglects available theory and evidence, or is guided by theoretical models which have been seriously criticised and largely replaced by more satisfactory models. Psychologists and other behavioural scientists have not necessarily made these models available beyond discipline-based publications, making such models inaccessible. In addition, failures within psychology to reconcile social-cognitive and behavioural models have increased the difficulty of the task.

Interventions need to be not only well designed, but also well described and characterised in order to ensure that unsuccessful methods are not repeated and that, where significant benefit is achieved, the benefit can be replicated. Such descriptions should cover both the behaviour of patients or members of the public and the behaviour of health professionals, as both may contribute to behaviour change and to health outcomes.

Interpretation of findings can be controversial and potentially subject to *post hoc* bias. This problem might be minimised if the size of finding to be considered valuable, rather than simply statistically significant, were specified in advance of data being available.

Population-based interventions in behavioural risk factors are complex, both in terms of the research processes and in terms of the simultaneous application of biomedical and behavioural science. It is therefore crucial that they are informed by the best available evidence from both sciences.

Acknowledgements

I am grateful to Theresa Marteau, Hannah McGee, Wendy Simpson, Sheina Orbell and Charles Abraham for discussions contributing to the ideas presented here.

References

1   Kanfer FH, Gaelick-Buys. Self-management methods. In: Kanfer FH, Goldstein AP (eds). 1991. *Helping People Change*. New York: Pergamon.

2   Michie S, Johnston M, Cockroft A, Ellinghouse C, Gooch C. 1995. Uptake and impact of health screening for hospital staff. *Journal of Organizational Behavior*; 16; 1: 85-92.

3   Cockroft A, Gooch C, Ellinghouse C, Johnston M, Michie S. 1994. Evaluation of a programme of health measurements and advice among hospital staff. *Occupational Medicine*; 44; 2: 70-76.

4   Perry CL, Kelder SH, Klepp K-I. 1994. Community-wide cardiovascular disease prevention in young people: Long-term outcomes of the Class of 1989 Study. *European Journal of Public Health*; 4: 188-194.

5   Rogers RW. 1975. A protection motivation theory of fear appeals and attitude change. *Journal of Psychology*; 91: 93-114.

6   Rogers RW. Cognitive and physiological processes in fear appeals and attitude change: A revised theory of Protection Motivation. In: Cacioppo JT, Petty RE (eds). 1983. *Social Psychophysiology: a Sourcebook*. New York: Guildford Press.

7   Bandura A. 1989. Perceived self-efficacy in the exercise of personal agency. *The Psychologist*; 2: 411-424.

8   Weiner B. 1988. Attribution theory and attributional therapy: some theoretical observations and suggestions. *British Journal of Clinical Psychology*; 27: 99-104

9   Schwarzer R. Self-efficacy in the adoption and maintenance of health behaviours: Theoretical approaches and a new model. In: Schwarzer R (ed). 1992. *Self-efficacy: Thought Control of Action*. London: Hemisphere.

10 Becker MH. 1974. The health belief model and sick role behaviour. *Health Education Monographs*; 2: 409-419.

11 Janz NK, Becker MH. 1984. The health belief model: a decade later. *Health Education Quarterly*; 11: 1-47.

12 Harrison JA, Mullen PD, Green LW. 1992. A meta-analysis of studies of the health belief model with adults. *Health Education Research*; 7: 107-116.

13 Fishbein M, Azjen I. 1975. *Belief, Attitude, Intention, and Behaviour*. New York: Wiley.

14 Fishbein M. Persuasive communication: a social-psychological perspective on factors influencing communication effectiveness. In: Bennett AE (ed). 1976. *Communication between Doctors and Patients*. Oxford: Oxford University Press.

15 Azjen I. 1988. *Attitudes, Personality and Behaviour*. Milton Keynes: Open University Press.

16 Sheppard BH, Hartwick J, Warshaw PR. 1988. The theory of reasoned action: A meta-analysis of past research with recommendations for modifications and future research. *Journal of Consumer Research*; 15: 325-339.

17 Prochaska JO, DiClemente CD. 1983. Stages and processes of self-change of smoking: Toward an integrative model of change. *Journal of Consulting and Clinical Psychology*; 51: 390-395.

18 DiClemente CD, Prochaska JO, Fairhurst SK, Velicer WF, Velasquez MM, Rossi JS. 1991. The process of smoking cessation: An analysis of precontemplation, contemplation, and preparation stages of change. *Journal of Consulting and Clinical Psychology*; 59: 295-304.

19 Marcus BH, Owen N. 1992. Motivational readiness, self-efficacy and decision-making for exercise. *Journal of Applied Psychology*; 22: 3-16.

20 Marcus BH, Rakowski W, Rossi JS. 1992. Assessing motivational readiness and decision making for exercise. *Health Psychology*; 11: 257-261.

21 Weinstein ND. 1988. The precaution adoption process. *Health Psychology*; 7: 355-386.

22 Weinstein ND, Sandman PM. 1992. Evidence from home radon testing. *Health Psychology*; 11: 170-180.

23 Gollwitzer PM. Goal achievement: the role of intentions. In: Stroebe W, Hewstone M (eds). 1993. *European Review of Social Psychology*; volume 4.

24 Orbell S, Hopkins S. 1994. It's easy to change behaviour if you know when to: implementation intentions and behavioural enactment. Paper delivered at the British Psychological Society Special Group in Health Psychology Annual Conference, September 1994.

25 Marteau TM, Johnston M. 1990. Health professionals: a source of variance in patient outcomes. *Psychology and Health*; 5: 47-58.

26 Schuker B, Wittes JT, Cutler JA, Bailey K, Mackintosh DR, Gordon DJ, Haines CM, Mattson ME, Goor RS, Rifkind BM. 1987. Changes in physician perspective on cholesterol and heart disease: Results from two national surveys. *Journal of the American Medical Association*; 258: 3521-3526.

27 Bekker H, Marteau TM. 1994. The role of health professionals' beliefs and attitudes in uptake of screening. Paper delivered at British Psychological Society Special Group in Health Psychology Annual Conference, September 1994.

28 Ley P. 1988. *Communicating with Patients*. London: Croom Helm.

29 Rudd P, Price MG, Graham LE, Beilstein BA, Tarbell SJH, Bacchetti P, Fortmann SP. 1986. Consequences of worksite hypertension screening. *American Journal of Medicine*; 80: 853-861.

30 Family Heart Study Group. 1994. Randomised controlled trial evaluating cardio-vascular screening and intervention in general practice: principal results of the British Family Heart Study. *British Medical Journal*; 308: 313-320.

31 Imperial Cancer Research Fund OXCHECK Study Group. 1994. Effectiveness of health checks conducted by nurses in primary care: results of the OXCHECK Study after one year. *British Medical Journal*; 308: 308-312.

32 British Medical Journal. 1994. *British Medical Journal*: 308: 285-286 and 852-853.

33 Beevers M, Curzio, J. 1994. Pessimism is uncalled for. *British Medical Journal*; 308: 853.

34 Johnston M, Vogele C. 1993. Benefits of psychological preparation for surgery: a meta-analysis. *Annals of Behavioral Medicine*; 15: 245-256.

Interventions among 'high-risk' populations in primary care

Professor Desmond Julian

Chairman, National Heart Forum

The term 'high-risk' in this section refers to individuals who have already manifested coronary heart disease (CHD) in the form of angina pectoris or myocardial infarction, or both. While it would clearly be preferable to prevent CHD manifesting itself in the first place, patients with these disorders are a very important group for the following reasons:

- They are numerous, amounting to some 2-3 million people.

- About 50% of deaths from CHD occur in those who have already been diagnosed with this disorder. Preventive measures which reduce mortality in this population would have a substantial effect on total deaths from CHD.

- Several strategies (beta-blockade, aspirin, ACE inhibitors and lipid-lowering) have been shown in randomised controlled trials to be effective in reducing mortality long-term in selected groups of post-infarction patients.

- These therapies have been shown not only to reduce mortality, but also to reduce morbidity, recurrent myocardial infarction, and the need for further hospitalisation.

- Lifestyle changes - in smoking cessation, physical activity and diet - have beneficial effects in patients with CHD but have been less studied by randomised clinical trials.

- Those in primary care have an essential role in ensuring that patients receive appropriate care. The primary care team should check patients' adherence to the lifestyle changes and therapeutic interventions as these are often not maintained.

Effective interventions after myocardial infarction

Cigarette smoking

There has been no randomised study of smoking cessation after myocardial infarction but several observational studies have shown that the mortality over the succeeding years is about 50% less in those who quit compared with those who continue to smoke. A study from Gothenburg, Sweden, reported that the mortality rate at five years was 14% in those who stopped smoking, compared with 29% in those who continued. The rates at 7.5 years were 16% and 49% respectively.[1]

Physical activity

An overview of clinical trials has suggested that rehabilitation with exercise after myocardial infarction can lead to a reduction in overall mortality of 20%-25%,[2] but it is difficult to say whether this effect is due to physical activity alone or to other beneficial lifestyle changes that tend to accompany it. Nonetheless, patients need to be encouraged to exercise within their limitations.

Diet

No large trials have been undertaken to determine whether dietary modification improves prognosis in those with CHD. One small trial with a very strict lipid-lowering regimen produced a borderline reduction in total cardiovascular events.[3] Another randomised trial reported that a diet containing fatty fish reduced recurrent infarction and death.[4] Patients with ischaemic heart disease should be encouraged to eat a diet with a low saturated fat content, and to increase their consumption of fruit, vegetables and fatty fish.

Lipid-lowering

The first conclusive evidence that lipid-lowering reduces overall mortality has been provided by the Scandinavian Simvastatin Survival Study (The 4S trial).[5] In this trial 4,444 patients with angina and/or previous myocardial infarction and a raised cholesterol level of 5.5-8.0mmol (in spite of a lipid-lowering diet) were randomised to receive simvastatin or placebo for a minimum period of five years. There was a 30% reduction in overall mortality (from 11.5% to 8.2%), a 42% reduction in coronary deaths, and highly significant reductions in other cardiovascular deaths (including stroke), in non-fatal myocardial infarction, and in the need for coronary bypass surgery. There were no serious side-effects and, in particular, there was no evidence to support the previous concerns that lipid-lowering might cause an increase in cancer and in violent death.

Although the full implications of this trial have yet to be evaluated (especially with regard to health economics), there is no doubt that its findings should be applied to post-infarction patients, many of whom are under the care of their GP and no longer attend hospital. All patients who have sustained a myocardial infarction should have their lipid levels analysed. If these are raised, a lipid-lowering diet should be prescribed. If this fails, consideration should be given to prescribing lipid-lowering drugs.

Control of diabetes
Diabetics who have sustained a myocardial infarction have an increased short-term and long-term risk of recurrent infarction and death. Good control of the diabetes is important in preventing further complications.

Anticoagulants and aspirin
It has been established in a number of clinical trials that both anticoagulants[6] (such as warfarin) and aspirin[7] are effective in reducing the risk of recurrent myocardial infarction and death. Because of the greater risk of bleeding and the problems of anticoagulant control, aspirin is regarded as the preferred option and is indicated in all CHD patients for whom there are no contraindications. Primary care has an important role here as many patients have never attended or no longer attend hospital; in such cases this therapy needs to be initiated by the GP.

Beta-blockers
Randomised controlled clinical trials have established that beta-blockers reduce mortality and reinfarction rates by 20%-25% in the months and years following myocardial infarction.[8] Some physicians recommend beta-blockers for all patients for whom they are not contraindicated. Others reserve the use of these drugs for those who have had a complicated course, or who have readily induced myocardial ischaemia, because it has been found that beta-blockers have little effect in those at low risk.[9]

Calcium antagonists and nitrates
Although these drugs have an important place in the treatment of angina, there is no evidence that they reduce mortality after infarction.

ACE inhibitors
ACE inhibitors reduce mortality in patients who have suffered from heart failure during the acute event,[10] or who have a reduced left ventricular function as assessed by echocardiography or nuclear imaging.[11] These agents should certainly be used long-term in those who are

in heart failure in the convalescent period, but are also indicated in those whose heart failure has been brought under control.

Overall preventive strategy after myocardial infarction
The recommended lifestyle measures - no smoking, dietary changes, and physical activity - are appropriate for all patients. It is probable that the various regimens described above are, at least to some extent, additive in their effects. Aspirin therapy is indicated for about 90% of post-infarction patients, beta-blockade for 30%-50%, and ACE inhibitors for about 20%. At present, it is uncertain what proportion of patients should receive lipid-lowering drugs.

Effective interventions in angina pectoris

Few trials have been undertaken in patients with angina, but it is reasonable to suppose that benefits would accrue from lifestyle changes, such as smoking cessation, dietary modifications, and increased physical activity within the patient's limitations.

Aspirin has been shown to be effective in reducing the incidence of myocardial infarction and death in patients with angina.[8] The 4S trial showed that lipid-lowering reduced mortality and morbidity in anginal patients with raised lipids.[5] Many patients with angina have not been assessed with regard to the potential benefit of these therapies and it is important that the primary care team identify all such individuals and initiate treatment when appropriate.

Implications for primary care

- Interventions by the primary care team can have an important effect on improving the prognosis of patients with CHD and thereby improving mortality figures overall.

- There is evidence that there are many unrecognised cases of CHD in the community, especially among women.

- There is good evidence that the management of patients with CHD in the community leaves much to be desired, particularly bearing in mind the effectiveness of the therapies that have been subjected to randomised controlled trials.

- Many patients in primary care have not been reviewed with regard to the potential benefits of these interventions. Furthermore, when appropriate interventions have been started, either in hospital or in the community, they have not been adhered to in the longer term. The primary care team has a responsibility to ensure that therapy, if indicated, is maintained.

References

1   Aberg A, Bergstrand R, Johansson S et al. 1983. Cessation of smoking after myocardial infarction. Effects on mortality after 10 years. *British Heart Journal*; 49: 416-422.

2   O'Connor GT, Buring JE, Yusuf S et al. 1989. An overview of randomized trials of rehabilitation with exercise after myocardial infarction. *Circulation*; 80: 234-244.

3   Watts GF, Lewis B, Brunt JN et al. 1992. Effects of coronary artery disease of lipid-lowering diet, or diet plus cholestyramine, in the St Thomas' Atherosclerosis Regression Study (STARS). *Lancet*: 339; 563-569.

4   Burr ML, Fehily AM, Gilbert JF et al. 1989. The effects of changes in fat, fish and fibre intakes on death and myocardial infarction: diet and reinfarction trial. *Lancet*; ii: 757-781.

5   The Scandinavian Simvastatin Survival Study Group. 1994. Randomised trial of cholesterol lowering in 4444 patients with coronary heart disease: the Scandinavian Simvastatin Survival Study (4S). *Lancet*; 344: 1383-1389.

6   Smith P, Arnesen H, Holme I. 1990. The effect of warfarin on mortality and reinfarction after myocardial infarction. *New England Journal of Medicine*; 323: 147-152.

7   Antiplatelet Trialists' Collaboration. 1994. Collaborative overview of randomised trials of antiplatelet therapy. Prevention of death, myocardial infarction, and stroke by therapy in various categories of patients. *British Medical Journal*; 308: 81-106.

8   Yusuf S, Peto R, Lewis J, Collins R, Sleight P. 1985. Beta-blockade during and after myocardial infarction: an overview of the randomized trials. *Prog Cardiovasc Dis*; 27: 335-371.

9   Furberg CD, Hawkins CM, Lichstein F. 1983. Effect of propranolol in postinfarction patients with mechanical and electrical complications. *Circulation*; 69: 761.

10   AIRE (Acute Infarction Ramipril Efficacy) Investigators. 1993. Effect of ramipril on mortality and morbidity of survivors of acute myocardial infarction with clinical evidence of heart failure. *Lancet*; 342: 821-828.

11   Pfeffer MA, Braunwald E, Moye LA, Basta L, Brown EJ, Cuddy TE et al. 1992. Effect of captopril on mortality and morbidity in patients with left ventricular dysfunction after myocardial infarction. *New England Journal of Medicine*; 327: 669-677.

Introducing screening programmes in primary care

Fedelma Winkler

Chief Executive, Kent Family Health Services Authority

The methods for introducing service changes to primary care must be designed to fit into current structures. This section outlines the key characteristics of these structures and the methods used to introduce change to a practitioner-led service, and puts forward proposals for the future.

The structure of primary care

The unique feature of primary care is that most of it is provided by 'independent contractors' working within an archaic small business structure and culture. It is archaic because each practice is a partnership - an organisational system suited to the delivery of service by autonomous professionals. This organisational system has persisted despite the increase in the number of partners and employees, and in the number and complexity of tasks now being undertaken in general practice. General practice has failed to develop the infrastructure to meet the changed circumstances.

Another feature of general practice is its variability, which is crucial when considering changes in policy. The size of delivery unit varies from the solo doctors with part-time receptionists to the 16-partner practices with associated professionals and support staff. There are patterns to these variations. The solo practising with little participation from other professionals is more frequently found in areas of social deprivation. Conversely, the 'team practices' in high quality premises are most likely to be found in areas of higher social class.

The quality of the service provided by general practice is unpredictable. The proportion of practices providing high quality service may be 20%

or 80% of the practices in an area. These assessments are at best based on very crude measures or, more usually, intuition.

The practice performance against targets for screening is a frequently used surrogate for a quality indicator. Other measures include prescribing habits, services offered, quality of premises, size, or numbers of night visits. Even these crude measures are not applied consistently nor used to inform decisions on developments.

Variations cannot be explained by resource allocation. GPs have had a national contract which, until 1990, gave them equal access to funds.

The other providers of primary care work in the managed environment of NHS Trusts. Change within those services can be effected within the management hierarchy or by organisational restructuring.

Programmes that require cooperation across the divide cause friction. Health visitors, for example, resent increasing GPs' income when they immunise children. Thought has to be given to the dove-tailing of the changes into the other sectors of primary care. The responsibility between the GP and community services has to be clearly defined. It also helps if there is consensus on the perceived benefits.

Any programme which is to be implemented in primary care has to be capable of being introduced in 11,000 small businesses with widely differing capacities and little accountability.

Commissioning primary care

In other sectors of health care, the purchaser-provider split is the main vehicle for change. General practice remains outside that system.

Primary care has four 'commissioners'. This is a source of fragmentation and rivalry.

- *The Department of Health* is the monopoly buyer of general medical services. It 'purchases' by paying a capitation fee for each patient on the GP's list. It also negotiates fees for specific services and adds to the package subsidies for premises, staff and education. Management of the contract is by reference to the Red Book with little regard to local need or quality of service provided.

- *Health Authorities* commission community health services. Their choice of provider is limited.

- *General Practitioner Fundholders* purchase community health services direct from providers. They can choose the provider as well as the services.

- *Family Health Services Authorities* administer the national contract, have limited monitoring functions and act as subsidiary commissioner for training and service developments.

Unless changes are made to the national contract, in the short to medium term primary care will continue to have multiple 'purchasers' and those seeking to introduce change will face that complexity.

How should screening programmes be introduced in primary care?

The future of primary care will be led by GPs. The introduction of service developments is therefore dependent on GPs, their organisational arrangements and the national contract negotiations.

The factors that influence professional behaviour are:

- user expectations

- professional commitment

- professional education

- financial incentives

- monitoring and feedback, and

- organisational arrangements.

All these factors are interdependent. Change in professional behaviour will most successfully be achieved by systems that integrate them.

User expectations
Patterns in service delivery exist in communities of different socioeconomic status. This suggests that user expectation is a significant factor, but not one that is easily manipulable.

In the development of screening, users have been a significant force. Cervical and breast screening were funded and national screening introduced because of the support of user groups. However, the groups most at risk were not captured because of the poor development of general practice in the areas of greatest need.

Professional commitment
The provision of quality service is motivated by personal values, concern for the community, professional pride, positive feedback, status among peers, and personal sense of worth. There is a particular irony in that those general practices with the most developed services are often not income-maximisers. This is because of the insensitivity of the nationally negotiated pricing system to quality. Financial incentives are frequently used to spread a particular activity from the leading edge practices to the majority. This fails to recognise that the reason for their success in the first place was the high motivation and organisation of the developing practices.

Policies for introducing change rarely consider how commitment and self-worth are affected by change. Too many changes, at too frequent intervals, may actually destroy commitment.

Professional education
Commitment to professional values is associated with an educational approach to change. In general practice, the kite-flyer for this approach is the Royal College of General Practitioners. One-third of GPs are members of the Royal College.

Resources are allocated annually from the public purse to support the continuing education of GPs and their staff.

Continuing education is not connected to the needs of the individual, the practice or service requirements. More significantly, this education occurs within occupational groups, and so actually hinders the development of integrated services.

Each service review calls for programmes to educate the GP and practice nurse. Every time a problem is exposed, further training is a major recommendation.

There is, however, no evidence that education alone effects significant changes or improves standards.

Financial incentives
Sixty per cent of a GP's income is from capitation payments. Much of the rest is derived from 'item of service' fees. Significant change in general practice takes place whenever the pricing structure is altered. Not surprisingly, in a section of the profession with a strong small business ethos, this is a favourite method for introducing change.

For the first time, the 1990 GP Contract included general health promotion as part of general medical services:

"The services which a doctor is required ... to render shall include the following:-
(a) giving advice, where appropriate, to a patient in connection with the patient's general health, and in particular about the significance of diet, exercise, the use of tobacco, the consumption of alcohol and the misuse of drugs and solvents."[1]

In addition, health promotion clinics, child health surveillance, immunisation and cervical cytology, were priced separately. These activity-related fees altered the balance of work in many practices.

Health promotion clinics
When the new GP contract was first introduced in 1990, GPs received a fee for every 10 patients they saw in a health promotion clinic. This produced a dramatic increase in health promotion clinics. However, the significant resources channelled into it brought little health gain.

Instead of giving health promotion advice as part of the normal consultation, patients were channelled into the fee-attracting clinics. Alternatively, all consultations became health promotion clinics.

For some practices, it was a bonanza. They aimed for maximum financial gain with minimum additional input. The practices that failed to gain economically were those who questioned the efficacy of this form of intervention or who refused to allow their priorities to be altered by the financial incentives.

The health promotion clinic payments were the most ill thought out of the fees-for-services. They were difficult for the new FHSAs to approve or monitor. They generated much activity, but their benefit was largely financial for the GPs.

The effect of the retrenchment on the health promotion programme remains with us. Those practices that put much work into developing quality programmes felt cheated when resources were withdrawn. Practices are now more wary of making significant changes without long-term commitments to funding.

The conversion of this scheme to the current three-band system (see Appendix 1) is a considerable improvement. GPs are rewarded on a population base for incorporating health screening into their normal consultations. But the same problems of definitions, quality, and monitoring remain.

Other consequences
The financial incentives caused a dramatic increase in the numbers of practice nurses. They became income earners for the practices. Much of the health promotion was delegated to them. Many of them had no previous experience of working in the community and no training in health promotion or screening. Some practices recruited nurses for the first time to do work not previously done in the practice. Many recruited the least trained nurses on a part-time basis and paid them little.

The drawback to financial incentives is that they do not guarantee that the professional is competent to undertake the procedure. The various scandals around cervical cytology were the result of the fee structure that did not require proof of competence.

Financial incentives can stimulate dramatic change quickly. The pitch of the price is crucial. If the reimbursement is too high, it can damage other services and attract people with no interest or competence in the work. If the price is too low, the service itself may suffer. For example, contraceptive services have become a prescribing activity because there is little financial incentive to offer a comprehensive service.

The fee-for-service is the quickest way to change activity levels in general practice, but on its own it is no guarantee of service quality. It is also highly expensive to administer and monitor effectively.

Monitoring and feedback
The 1990 reforms introduced, for the first time, monitoring, audit and feedback as instruments of change.

The monitoring systems previously in place were financial. Family Practitioner Committees (FPCs) had poor to non-existent information systems. What monitoring systems they did have concentrated on fraudulent claims.

When the financial incentives were extended, FPCs had few systems in place to check on competency of practices to undertake the procedures. They had no monitoring or review systems at all. More importantly, they did not have a culture of concern for quality of services.

Prescribing

A major investment following the reforms was in monitoring GP prescribing. The positive effect of monitoring and feedback is visible. Prescribing is the one area in primary care that has excellent data. There is also a consensus on what is good prescribing. Medical and prescribing advisers, therefore, have good information to feed back to practitioners on their individual performance and how they compare with their peers. Advisers are also able to track the impact which information has on the prescribing habits of individual practitioners.

This method is effective in bringing change in behaviour, but is time-consuming and costly. It relies heavily on the technical and persuasive skills of the advisers. A cost-benefit analysis is needed to see if it is more cost-effective than financial incentives alone.

The greatest change takes place when prescribing monitoring is combined with financial incentives. There is, however, some evidence that the change is only sustained for the period that the financial incentive is in operation.

Health promotion

There are problems with the health promotion banding scheme, including poor follow-up and lack of clear feedback to practices. The benefits of obtaining population-based data have been subordinated to the clinical freedom of the independent contractors. For example, the World Health Organization's definition of hypertension was accepted as standard, but GPs are allowed to use another provided that they tell the FHSA which one they are using. These variations make it virtually impossible to monitor the scheme effectively.

Organisational arrangements

The rest of the NHS believes that organisational change is necessary to get changes in service delivery. The purchaser-provider split is the current engine for driving change. The organisational arrangements in general practice remain unchanged.

GPs have been contractors since 1948. The contract was renegotiated in the 1960s and again in 1990. Major changes followed each.

The 1990 contract attempted, for the first time, to introduce a system of local accountability to general practice. This was to be the responsibility of the Family Practitioner Committees (FPCs).

In 1991, Family Health Services Authorities were charged with changing the culture of their predecessor organisations, the FPCs. They were expected to be proactive, not reactive, in their relationship to general practice. They were required to take account of the needs of the local communities in planning services and not just those of the GPs. They had little preparation or specific training for taking on such a fundamental shift in function. Similarly, no advance planning had been undertaken as to the technical support necessary for the change in role, such as management information systems. The information software necessary for monitoring and making payments was commissioned only after programmes had been implemented.

Furthermore, all local developments had to be within the straightjacket of the nationally agreed contract. This contract relinquishes a key lever, the selection of providers. The overwhelming majority of GPs coming on to the contractor list are selected by existing GPs as partners. Practices recruit their own partners to meet their needs. There is no requirement on them to have regard for any wider considerations.

Once on the contractor list, the GP can only be removed from it by a costly and rarely used application to the NHS Tribunal. This contrasts sharply with the systems in the Community Health Services. They moved into trusts with emphasis on fitness-for-function, performance appraisal, and the use of short-term contracts for increasing numbers of staff.

Locally agreed contracts
Experiments have taken place which give contracts to practices to provide new services, to extend existing services, or to enable practices to contract with others to provide a service. Local contracts can be an additional instrument for change and a vehicle for bringing together all the instruments.

Contracts for new services. In Kent, for example, 60 contracts have been entered into by practices for the provision of counselling services. These contracts are with a preferred provider, able to meet the quality and supervisory requirements and provide a service of the required standard. This enables a professional counselling service to be offered to half a million people through their GP. The 'mother contract' was negotiated and priced by the FHSA, with GPs agreeing practice contracts with the provider.

Existing services brought into contract. As part of the Barking and Havering Joint Commissioning Project, a system for contracting with

GPs for the provision of comprehensive contraceptive services was developed.

Using a 'zero based commissioning' approach, the volume and types of services required to meet local needs were identified. Contracts for the provision of services were placed with providers who could fulfil the specifications. Before contracts were placed, considerable work was undertaken to identify quality providers. As access for the whole population was a requirement, the FHSA supported providers with experience and with an interest in developing to meet the specifications of the contracts. The educational institutions were encouraged to adapt courses to meet the needs of the new service.

The contracts for the enhanced comprehensive contraceptive clinics were given to the voluntary sector, an NHS Trust and practices. The service was integrated across the providers by unified commissioning. The FHSA thus capitalised on existing good services and was able to offer guarantees to patients about the level and quality of the service they could expect from accredited clinics. Practices without the skills, facilities or inclination were not given contracts. They were, however, given a standard and the offer of help to achieve that standard, so that in future they could come into the accredited system.

The drawback to this approach is the amount of investment needed to enable practices to reach the desired standard, and the ongoing support needed to maintain commitment.

In developing the service, the FHSA used all the levers for change outlined above. It sought practices with motivation, set up special training for staff, agreed financial rewards, and introduced an auditing and monitoring system that was agreed by all. It involved users in providing feedback. And it used the contracting process as the organisational vehicle for change.

Time scales. This type of programme succeeds only if the local contractor and the providers work jointly over a considerable period of time and build trust and continuous development into the process.

A problem for locally agreed contracts is the mobility of the contract negotiators in contrast to the immobility of the providers. Practitioners spend a lifetime in a community yet are expected to trust the good will of managers who, in the current climate, may not be in an area for longer than two years.

Senior managers in the NHS have been trained for managing hospitals. Their training will not have included the management of clinicians. General management itself was only introduced less than 10 years ago. NHS organisations are also characterised by the rigid hierarchical structures. This training and structure do not breed the characteristics needed to negotiate contracts with professional small businesses. Developing good local contracts requires staff who are knowledgeable and flexible and who carry responsibility. That requires a shallow hierarchical structure.

Conclusion

Working with providers so that services are tailored via contracts to the needs of the community requires giant leaps by commissioners. For many managers it means ceding control to users and professionals at a time when culturally they have come to expect more control. Education is needed to enable them to manage through motivation, contracts, negotiation, and sponsoring development.

The screening programme to be introduced and the intervention expected from primary care needs to build on the lessons of the past:

- GPs must be convinced that the intervention is of value to their patient.

- Strong professional commitment will be necessary.

- Educational programmes need to be designed to accompany the change.

- Fees need to be negotiated that are fair and acknowledged to be fair.

- The distortions that are likely to occur need to be projected. What are the unintended consequences of paying a specific fee? What impact will it have on utilisation? Is this harmful? Will the system be monitored? What impact will it have on the other primary care providers?

- Before obtaining any allowance, practices should complete an assessed training programme and show commitment to the programme.

- Resources should be allocated to support development locally, to ensure that those areas most in need have accredited practitioners.

- Feedback on performance to the practitioners needs to be part of the contracting process.

- The cost and most appropriate ways of monitoring have to form part of the planning process and the resource allocation.

- Appropriate training programmes for those responsible for implementation and monitoring should be part of the strategy and should take place before the programme has been implemented, not developed when problems arise.

- Users and potential users must be informed of the standards expected of providers.

- There must be clear, enforceable sanctions for those failing to meet the agreed standard.

In the future, it is possible that health authorities may become the commissioners of all primary care. This would mean general practice being brought into locally agreed contracts for the provision of general medical services and for any specialist services they wish to provide. The method might be different, but the levers would remain similar.

The Department of Health did not take advantage of its monopoly position in a market of small providers. The result was that the financial incentives were crude instruments to get the action from the poorest performers. This distracted from the holistic generalist nature of primary care and trapped too many GPs into the small business mentality.

A contract system designed to entice the best with emphasis on professional service and priced for service and quality might in the end give patients better guarantees of standards.

Reference

1   Department of Health. 1989. *Terms of Service for Doctors in General Practice. November 1989.* London: Department of Health.

Implications for the future: a personal view

Dr Alistair Cameron

National Health Service Executive, Department of Health

In seeking to answer the question 'Where are we now in cardiovascular prevention in primary care?' it is worth bearing in mind the following points.

Firstly, the health promotion banding system in general practice, which is the cornerstone of the government's coronary heart disease (CHD) and stroke prevention policy in primary care, already exists. It cannot be re-invented from scratch, and there would need to be very powerful evidence to lead the Department of Health to abandon it altogether.

However, the *British Medical Journal* editorial which accompanied the publication of the OXCHECK Study and the British Family Heart Study described the banding system in primary care as "blanket" health promotion and a "waste of resources". Policy makers are, therefore, duty bound to examine carefully the evidence which supports such statements.

Secondly, it is worth stressing that the health promotion banding system in the current GP contract is a flexible system. Although Band 3, in particular, has been widely criticised, the criteria (given in Appendix 1) offer a very flexible framework within which primary health care teams can operate. The Family Health Services Authority (FHSA), after consulting with the Local Medical Committee on how to apply the criteria, will approve a health promotion programme if it is satisfied that:
- the proposed content of the programme is in accordance with modern, authoritative medical opinion, and

- the coverage level proposed is appropriate.
The associated guidance issued to FHSAs is also flexible.

Data collection

Before embarking on health promotion activities, it is first necessary to establish whether any cardiovascular risk factor needs to be changed. If a need is established, then its presence or absence should be recorded. If a specific intervention is carried out to meet a need - perhaps a readiness to change or the existence of multiple risk factors - then that data should also be recorded.

This is the basis of good record-keeping and good communication between different members of the primary health care team. Not only does it allow other people involved in the care of the patient to intervene as and when appropriate in accordance with modern authoritative medical opinion; it also facilitates audit.

Data collection is not meaningless. It would be impossible to run an effective programme of cervical cytology screening or immunisation without adequate recording, storage, and retrieval of the relevant data. Data collection is meaningless only if the person conducting the activity perceives it as valueless.

However, it is important to examine the value of each piece of information which is being collected and to ask whether using these data in Annual Reports to the FHSA is the best method of ensuring accountability for the substantial sums of public money which are being invested in the health promotion programme.*

What constitutes conclusive evidence in relation to prevention in primary care?

An analogy has been drawn between health promotion and an infant (see Chapter 3, page 28). The health promotion banding system has been conceived, delivered and is already in its infancy. There is, therefore, little point in debating the quality of the pre-conceptual counselling. Both the General Medical Services Committee (GMSC) and the Department of Health, like many parents, did their best given the evidence available at the time. But it is important to examine whether

---

* *Since the expert meeting, the NHS Executive has examined these issues, taking into consideration the views expressed at the meeting. (See footnote on page 5.)*

the health promotion programme, as laid out in the Red Book and the associated guidance, suffers from a congenital abnormality which could prove to be fatal.

The question: 'Are antibiotics appropriate for sore throats?' has been debated in the *British Medical Journal*. The question could be rephrased as: 'What is the percentage reduction in life-threatening illness or serious morbidity which results from consultations for sore throats and prescriptions issued in relation to the latter?' Or: 'What are the costs and side-effects, and does all this activity have a satisfactory cost-benefit ratio?'

A Professor of Therapeutics responded:

"You would think that with all the resources going into medical research we would know whether antibiotics should routinely be used to treat sore throats. It is after all, a simple question about a common condition. Nevertheless, we simply do not know."

In summary, there was just not enough evidence to decide.

In an earlier *British Medical Journal* article on 'Recent advances in general practice', a Professor of General Practice stated that it may take a long time "for ineffective therapies or services to be removed from medical practice".

The OXCHECK Study and the British Family Heart Study were then used to justify a statement that "unselective screening of general practice populations is an ineffective way of significantly reducing cardiovascular risk."[1]

This led on to a statement that the risk factor reductions achieved "translate into only a 12% decline in the overall risk of coronary events among the population, which is very disappointing in a public health context."[1]

The purpose of comparing treatment of sore throats with lifestyle advice for prevention of CHD and strokes is to ask 'What constitutes conclusive evidence in respect of evaluating prevention through primary care?' This question is dealt with in more detail on page 28 by Professor McPherson, who also makes the point that:

"Successfully attributing effectiveness to interventions is generally complicated. In contrast to prevention policies, evaluating therapeutic treatments is systematically easier. This is because they are specific to the patient and his or her disease, and always administered by enthusiasts for the therapeutic role."

Another way of posing the question would be: 'If I was a highly sophisticated purchaser, given the stark option of choosing between treatment of sore throats with antibiotics and cardiovascular disease prevention, which would I choose on the basis of the evidence available?'

One could effectively avoid the question by saying: "Let the patient choose!" in the belief that the patient will prefer to have his or her sore throat treated by antibiotics rather than any effort being put into having his heart attack or stroke prevented. But how confident can we be that this is the view of the patient?

A research study in which patients were asked about smoking, physical activity, weight, and fitness issues, concluded that:

> "The findings of this study suggest that greater participation by GPs in health promotion would be well received by most patients and that currently there may be considerable discrepancies between patients' expectations and their perceptions of their GP's interest in these areas of preventive medicine."[2]

Great care must be taken before saying that patients do not want health promotion in primary care. If they do want it they would like to receive it from someone who believes that it may do some good. A relatively high proportion of health professionals simply do not regard disease prevention and health promotion as their vocation. This might and perhaps should change, if the evidence justifies it.

Where do we go from here?

There appear to be several options concerning what to do with our health promotion banding 'infant'.

The first is infanticide, on the basis that the baby is so ugly and unworthy that it would be a kindness to put it out of its misery.

The second is to opt for major change, perhaps by fostering the infant out to experts in secondary health care who feel that resources should be switched, for example, to managing already sick people (in this case people who already have cardiovascular disease) in the belief that the GMSC and the NHS Executive have been irresponsible parents.

The third is for all the infant's relatives to put aside their differences and to collectively nurture the child through childhood into adulthood in the hope that the infant's currently hidden talents will surprise everybody. This option would allow a more measured examination of what intervention other than drastic surgery is necessary to enhance health promotion in primary care.

Infanticide is a dramatic solution and the baby would have to be condemned beyond all reasonable doubt for this to happen. Fostering - the rejection of primary prevention in the absolute favour of secondary prevention - is not the best solution either.

If the 12% reduction in coronary risk achieved by the OXCHECK Study is 'quite encouraging' rather than 'very disappointing', then one might be provocative and ask why there has not been a significant *Health of the Nation*-related shift in resources towards primary care from the secondary care sector as a result of public health activity in purchasing authorities.

Is it possible that primary care advocates and leaders may have scored, or may be in danger of scoring, a spectacular own goal by denying their own success or potential for success in the field of achieving cardiovascular disease prevention?

It would be a great irony if, while we stand on the threshold of a primary care led NHS for the first time since it was formed, its advocates were to turn their backs on contributing to primary prevention.

References

1   Silagy C. Recent advances. General Practice. 1994. *British Medical Journal*: 309; 943-945.
2   Wallace PG, Haines AP. 1984. *British Medical Journal*: 289; 534-536.

Chapter 4

Response to the OXCHECK Study and the British Family Heart Study

Royal College of General Practitioners

Results

Results assessing the changes observed in the OXCHECK Study and British Family Heart Study were available at the end of one year. This would be considered a short span of time in behavioural terms for such a large group.

The OXCHECK Study

In the OXCHECK Study there was a small reduction in total cholesterol concentration in the intervention group - mainly in women. This was matched by a small decrease in the fat intake in the intervention group.

There was a small decrease in blood pressure but the significant component could be related to 'accommodation' or 'acclimatisation'. This effect has been observed in earlier trials. Within the intervention group, only 24 patients commenced hypotensive drugs within the year of the study, and 41 commenced treatment for hyperlipidaemia.

The outcome for smoking was disappointing: the study produced no significant difference. This is in contrast to previous trials of doctor-led advice and advice followed by the use of nicotine patches.

The British Family Heart Study

In the British Family Heart Study, change in the intervention group was measured by a reduction in the CHD risk score. This was found to be of the order of 16%. The difference was most marked at the top end of risk. The component risk factors themselves did not contribute equally. The reduction of blood pressure amounted to about half the observed reduction in risk, smoking one-third, and cholesterol a quarter.

However, it was felt that there was considerable bias and that some of the lowering of blood pressure could be attributed to accommodation. On this basis it was felt that the intervention would have only contributed to approximately half the observed reduction.

Of the smokers recruited, a significant proportion did not return at one year (12% of men, and 15% of women). It is also possible that those returning may have under-reported their smoking habits as has been observed in other trials.

The small amount of cholesterol reduction was probably not open to bias and was matched by a small weight loss. Within the returning group there was a disproportionately large number of people with low risk factors and a higher proportion with diagnosed hypertension, raised blood cholesterol, diabetes and CHD.

Comments

The authors of the British Family Heart Study commented that the sample covered in their study represented about one-sixth of the total average practice population eligible for the programme (presumably meaning the health promotion component of the GP contract covering ages 16-74), and that extending the programme to the whole population would require four full-time practice nurses.

Although both trials could be applied to general practice, the studies do not reflect the way general practice functions, since the health checks were carried out by specially trained practice nurses and there was no evidence of team work or of integration of the study within the activity of the practice.

The authors also conclude that the real reduction of coronary risk is not 16% but, owing to the bias, is more likely to be 12%. This, if extrapolated to the whole population, would produce only an 8% impact on CHD and death. The British Family Heart Study authors commented that it would probably be more sensible to focus limited primary care resources on high-risk patients such as those with hypertension, hyperlipidaemia, diabetes and established CHD, and that primary care cannot on its own provide a population approach to reducing risk of CHD, and others need to contribute.

The authors of the OXCHECK Study commented that there could be a danger in trying to change too many risk factors at once and, therefore, diluting important messages.

Concentrating on those with existing cardiovascular disease would probably be more effective, bearing in mind the high prevalence of this group in the general population.

This response was prepared by Dr John Noakes on behalf of the Royal College of General Practitioners. The RCGP is a member organisation of the National Heart Forum.

Response to the OXCHECK Study and the British Family Heart Study

Health Visitors' Association

The OXCHECK Study[1] and the British Family Heart Study[2] represent a welcome addition to the literature in evaluating approaches to health promotion. However, perhaps the biggest surprise about the rather unimpressive impact of the interventions, is that these results should be a surprise to anyone. The reaction of the media was to suggest that the results indicate that such interventions are pointless and as a result many have questioned the value of health promoting activities.

This critique will comment little on the methods used for the research, but will concentrate mainly on the methodology - that is, the entire system of philosophical assumptions which underpin the chosen approach - to explain both why the results might have been predicted, and to dispute the conclusions and proposals made in the final discussion.

Background to the studies

Both papers set the study in the context of the new GP contract but neither refer to any mainstream health promotion literature. A review of this would have revealed that the chosen interventions demonstrated features which have previously been tried and found wanting; Tannahill[3] described them as 'state of the ark practice, not state of the art'. The literature would also have prepared the researchers for the low attendance by those most 'at risk' and warned of the likelihood of non-returners.

Risk factors

No attempt was made to explore the meaning of 'health' in the papers, or to justify the relevance of the intervention other than in respect of reducing risk factors. The underlying assumption is clearly that 'health' is viewed, not merely as an absence of disease, but as an absence of risk factors. The British Family Heart Study Group notes the importance attached to these in the *Health of the Nation* strategy,[4] and states that the important question is whether intervention will result in a reduction of the risk factors.

For the target group, a more important question may be how relevant the risk factors seem to their own state of health, at the particular moment in time. This would be considered in an approach which took account of the need for an 'epidemiology of health'[3] rather than a focus on actual or potential disease alone. Risk factors may describe different patterns of health problems, but they do not explain the causes of the different patterns, which are often connected to social inequalities.[5] Little is known about the natural history of disease, and research in the general population demonstrates that subjectively good health often co-exists with an objectively demonstrable pathology, which is sometimes quite severe. (See reference 6 for a review of such studies.)

A large sample was selected according to age and gender in both the studies under review. However, although the OXCHECK group recorded the spread of social class, neither group made any attempt to explore the impact of this, or other potentially intervening variables such as income, poverty or caring responsibilities that are known to adversely influence the factors being targeted.[7-9] Similarly ignored were any positive, health-enhancing factors like social support or autonomy.[10, 11] These variables may well have outweighed the impact of the intervention.

Ethical issues

The risk factor approach emphasises the moral dimension of health, viewing illness as a kind of punishment for not following a 'proper' way of life.[5] It is closely linked to the 'traditional preventive' approach to health education which supports a paternalistic 'professional expert' view of health promotion.[12, 13] Linking preventive activities solely to disease rather than to health increases the professionalisation and medicalisation of everyday life.[14]

The use of a record booklet, *Your Passport to Health*, in the British Family Heart Study[2] to record 'progress' seems especially likely to imply that people need to be supervised in living their own lives. It is reminiscent of an old-fashioned school report, and may thus infantilise the client group. Furthermore, encouraging people to believe that following prescribed behaviours will guarantee health seems unethical. Conversely, implying that people cannot achieve health without medical approval, is more likely to impair rather than improve health in the long term, by undermining autonomy and increasing dependence.[6]

Within the present NHS market, we are all charged to measure outcomes. The approach of these studies is 'things measurable as hard data'. Thus a challenge has to be, 'Exactly what sort of changes did the authors anticipate from a nursing intervention of this type?' Was it an appropriate type of intervention and indeed other than in studies of smoking cessation what evidence is there that GP interventions would be 'more successful'? Ethically, what is success anyway? And is overall *cost-effectiveness* being confused with a type of intervention being *more effective*?

Inequalities

The OXCHECK Study permitted nurses to set priorities according to identified risk, and 'patients' were afforded a role in negotiating targets. However, there appears little recognition of the need to empower the research subjects to take autonomous decisions about their own health. Scant detail was given in either paper about how the nurses had been trained and by whom; a heavy emphasis seems to have been placed on risk calculation and instruction. Despite wide use of the terms 'counselling' and 'choice', the attitude conveyed is one of professionally dominant 'sick-nursing' rather than 'health-nursing'.[15]

This approach would be particularly likely to further disadvantage people with less education, those from minority ethnic or the lower socioeconomic groups, who are at greater statistical risk from coronary heart disease and who were less likely to attend or return in these studies. Self-empowerment is viewed as a central concept in health promotion, because it can help such disadvantaged groups,[13, 16] whereas population-based interventions focusing on single issues do not necessarily redress inequalities in health.[17]

Lifestyle

The term 'lifestyle' originally signified a concept which integrated social and cultural context, individual perceptions and subjectively determined actions into a single unified whole.[18] The usage in these papers has, instead, fractured the concept to indicate specific factors which make up one part of the way people live their lives. Fragmenting the context for health promotion in this way may set the scene for health-harming, professional-expert attitudes and victim blaming.[19]

The inclusion of both partners in the British Family Heart Study is a positive feature in that it retains part of the sociocultural context, and the longer timescale in the OXCHECK Study is more realistic in considering changes over three years, rather than in the very short time frame of one year. However, neither paper recorded for how long dietary changes or smoking cessation had been sustained. No recognition is given to the complexities of achieving changes in lifestyle nor to the detailed literature about the stages and processes involved.[20-22]

Nurses' views and activities relating to health promotion

Health visitors are specifically trained in health promotion. A study by the Social Policy Research Unit at York University showed that only 3% of practice nurses were health visitors.[23] Many practice nurses are aware that they lack knowledge in this area and require further education. The above mentioned study showed practice nurse involvement in 'general health promotion' to be around 90%. Furthermore, as yet unpublished work on practice nurses shows the wide variation in meaning of health promotion to practice nurses and that for a large majority it consists of identifying a problem such as raised blood pressure and giving out a leaflet. Another study has shown the lack of knowledge of practice nurses in the area of health promotion and the wish of such nurses to receive more training both in how to promote health and how to organise clinics.[24]

Conclusion

The OXCHECK Study and the British Family Heart Study were carried out at the time of a government initiative which essentially prescribed the nature and form of the intervention, in terms of the *Health of the Nation* strategy[4] and in the new conditions of service for GPs. Viewed in this context, there is little reason for either study to take cognisance of the wider implications for health for the client group; implementing the strategy and achieving the targets are what counts. The results in both studies were viewed as disappointing; the authors linked this to the fact that the interventions were carried out by nurses. Closer medical involvement was urged, on the grounds that interventions by GPs have proved to be helpful in the past. However, like doctors, nurses have demonstrated good results with helping people to stop smoking in a variety of different settings.[25]

As this critique suggests, the main fault lies not in the implementation of the approach alone, but in the underlying problematic assumption that health is best achieved by treating it like a disease. Early treatment, careful control and rehabilitation in cases of established disease are all a suitable focus for medical intervention, and a greater emphasis on empowering health promoting attitudes might improve outcomes in those situations.

Overall, these studies do not make a case for everyone to abandon health promotion, which continues to be needed to reduce inequalities and preventable suffering. Rather, they add to the growing literature which demonstrates the poor results achieved when a medical approach is used for these purposes. In maintaining health, medical intervention is not always the most effective way. Achieving a 'well population' requires a different attitude and mindset than that which currently prevails in today's NHS.

This response was prepared on behalf of the Health Visitors' Association by Dr Sarah Cowley of King's College, London, with support from Margaret Buttigieg, Director of the Health Visitors' Association and members of the HVA Professional and General Purposes Sub-Committee. The HVA is a member organisation of the National Heart Forum.

References

1   OXCHECK Study Group. 1994. Effectiveness of health checks conducted by nurses in primary care: results of the OXCHECK Study after one year. *British Medical Journal;* 308: 308-312.

2   Family Heart Study Group. 1994. Randomised controlled trial evaluating cardio-vascular screening and intervention in general practice: principal results of the British Family Heart Study. *British Medical Journal;* 308: 313-320.

3   Tannahill A. 1992. Epidemiology and health promotion: a common understanding. In: Bunton R, Macdonald G (eds). *Health Promotion: Disciples and Diversity.* London: Routledge.

4   Department of Health. 1992. *The Health of the Nation: A Strategy for Health in England.* London: HMSO.

5   Neihoff J, Schneider F. 1993. Epidemiology and the criticism of the risk-factor approach. In: Lafaille R, Fulder S (eds). *Towards a New Science of Health.* London: Routledge.

6   Rijke R. 1993. Health in medical science: from determinism towards autonomy. In: Lafaille R, Fulder S (eds). *Towards a New Science of Health.* London: Routledge.

7   Blackburn C. 1991. *Poverty and Health: Working with Families.* Milton Keynes: Open University Press.

8   Graham H. 1987. Women's smoking and family health. *Social Sciences and Medicine;* 25: 47-96.

9   Graham H. 1993. Women's smoking: Government targets and social trends. *Health Visitor;* 66: 60-82.

10 House J, Landis K, Umberson D. 1988. Social relationships and health. *Science;* 241: 540-545.

11 Rowe J, Kahn R. 1987. Human ageing: usual and successful. *Science*; 237: 143-149.

12 Downie R, Fyfe C, Tannahill A. 1990. *Health Promotion: Models and Values*. Oxford: Oxford Medical Publications.

13 Tones K, Tilford S, Robinson Y. 1990. *Health Education: Effectiveness and Efficiency*. London: Chapman and Hall.

14 Lafaille R, Hiemstra H. 1990. The regimen of Salerno: a contemporary analysis of a medieval lifestyle programme. *Health Promotion International*; 5: 57-74.

15 Macleod Clark J. 1993. From sick nursing to health nursing: evolution or revolution? In: Wilson-Barnett J, Macleod Clark J (eds). *Research in Health Promotion and Nursing*. Basingstoke: Macmillan.

16 World Health Organization. 1984. A discussion document on the concept and principles of health promotion. Reproduced in: *Health Promotion International*; 1; 1: 73-76.

17 Reading R, Colver A, Openshaw S, Jarvis S. 1994. Do interventions that improve immunisation uptake also reduce social inequalities in uptake? *British Medical Journal*; 308: 1142-1144.

18 Corell J, Levin J, Jaco E. 1985. Lifestyle: an emergent concept in the socio-medical sciences. *Culture, Medicine and Psychiatry*; 9: 423-437.

19 Cowley S. 1995. Health as process: a health visiting perspective. *Journal of Advanced Nursing*; 3: 433-441.

20 Bandura A. 1977. *Social Learning Theory*. Englewood Cliffs, New Jersey: Prentice Hall.

21 Becker MH. 1974. The Health Belief Model and Personal Health Behaviour. *Health Education Monographs*; 2: 324-508.

22 Prochaska J, DiClemente C. 1984. *The Transtheoretical Approach: Crossing Foundations of Change*. Homewood, Illinois: Dow Jones Irwin.

23 Atkin K, Lunt N, Parker G, Hirst M. 1993. *Nurses Count: A National Census of Practice Nurses*. York: Social Policy Research Unit, University of York.

24 Ross F, Bower L, Sibbald B. Practice nurses: characteristics, workload and training needs. *British Journal of General Practice*; 44: January 15-18.

25 Macleod Clark J, Dines A. 1993. Case studies of health promotion with adults: nurses working with people who wish to stop smoking. In: Dines A, Cribb A (eds). *Health Promotion Concepts and Practice*. Oxford: Blackwell Scientific Publications.

Response to the OXCHECK Study and the British Family Heart Study

Royal College of Nursing

The Royal College of Nursing welcomes the opportunity provided by the OXCHECK Study to reiterate the value of nursing in primary health care and health promotion.

The conclusions of the study have been reported as indicative of the failure of practice nurses to achieve health gain. However, those nurses achieved a remarkable 12% reduction in coronary heart disease risk over a one-year period. If the study had not restricted itself to a quantitative analysis based upon the sole criteria of blood pressure measurement and hypertension, other positive outcomes of nursing intervention would no doubt have been detected, such as those concerned with interaction and communication.

Other studies[1] have shown that nurses are adept in establishing rapport with their patients who subsequently use their consultation to consider a whole range of issues. Patients consistently report that a key benefit of consulting the nurse is the time and understanding given to them and the feeling of partnership in their health care.

While it may be necessary to use an empirical study such as the OXCHECK Study, it must be emphasised that using only limited physiological criteria as a measure of success in terms of nursing input to health gain is not sufficient.

It is recommended that the OXCHECK Study Group consider the adoption of an alternative research method designed to identify the qualitative input of nursing care, rather than the biomedical approach they chose to use.

Research tools designed to examine nursing outcomes would provide a totally different picture.

This response was prepared by Jane Naish and Mark Jones on behalf of the Royal College of Nursing. The RCN is a member organisation of the National Heart Forum.

Reference

1   Stilwell B et al. 1987. A nurse practitioner in general practice: working styles and pattern of consultation. *Journal of the Royal College of General Practitioners;* 37: 154-157.

Response to the OXCHECK Study and the British Family Heart Study

Association of Facilitators in Primary Care

Although the results of the OXCHECK Study and the British Family Heart Study originally appeared to be pessimistic, they did in fact support the direction of thought within most district health authorities that health promotion should be based on need, and that in order to assess need baseline data should be collected. The screening programme allows that process.

While it is important to identify areas of need, the general public should be allowed access to information which allows them to make lifestyle choices. When that process is completed the input by professionals should be proportional to need, and innovative ways used to address that need.

The initial press response to the results of the two studies made an objective interpretation of the studies very difficult. Contentious statements such as "£80 million wasted on health promotion", instantly made life harder for professionals who believe that management of change relating to lifestyle can ultimately improve individuals' health.

Many professionals would agree that the screening programme is part of health education which is merely one of the tools of health promotion, and indeed both studies support that. Although there had been some modification of lifestyle, the underlying issues of poverty, unemployment and housing still have to be addressed and should be part of a health promotion programme which is government-led and supported by health professionals.

It would be wrong to scrap the screening programme on the basis of these limited data. Both studies offered follow-up after only one year but the management of change, according to Prochaska and DiClemente[1] is cyclical and it may take many attempts before the behaviour change is permanent. Perhaps a more realistic time scale for follow-up would be 10 or 20 years. However, it would be difficult to identify which intervention was responsible for the change and therefore unsatisfactory for the researchers. Furthermore, when managing lifestyle change, only one behaviour should be addressed, an argument supported by the OXCHECK Study.

Neither of the two studies found a significant effect on the smoking status of patients and indeed other studies have shown that no intervention has been particularly effective. However, in the last 20 years, the prevalence of smoking among adults aged 16 and over has fallen, from 52% to 31% in males and from 41% to 29% in females.[2] Perhaps the raising of public awareness, discussion between patients and professionals, and concerted campaigns are responsible for that change. So although individual surgery data are not significant, such data are important in the larger perspective. Perhaps those still smoking are the people who would be affected by a change in government policy, namely a ban on tobacco advertising. The health professional has a responsibility to continue informing the patient who smokes of the dangers, and to support individuals in their efforts to stop.

Both the OXCHECK Study and the British Family Heart Study were considered effective in helping patients to modify their diet and lower cholesterol levels. The British Family Heart Study intervention also helped in lowering blood pressure. These effects were achieved by nurses whose training varied from two to three days (in the OXCHECK Study) to longer training of unspecified duration (in the British Family Heart Study), and who were then deposited within surgeries not necessarily working as part of the team. It would seem that the most appropriate use of skills is to have a team approach to any aspect of work within primary care.[3]

Both studies suggest that the health promotion package[4] is not justified in the format tested and doubtful in its new format.[5] Facilitators believe in the value of health promotion and that health education has its uses provided that it is part of a comprehensive programme.[6] There does not appear to be anything in either the OXCHECK Study or British Family Heart Study that disproves that standpoint.

Conclusions

- Data collection via screening is essential to identify areas of need.
- The general population should be enabled to make informed health choices.

- Media sensationalism relating to research reports is detrimental to the work of health professionals.

- Health education related to screening is just part of health promotion and should not be judged in isolation.

- Management of change is a continuum and one year is an insufficient length of time for follow-up.

- No single smoking intervention is considered particularly effective, and yet the prevalence of smoking continues to decline. A variety of approaches is therefore essential.

- Interventions relating to diet, blood cholesterol and blood pressure are deemed effective but not overtly acknowledged.

- The nurse should be part of the primary health care team rather than working in isolation.

- There is a need for a comprehensive health promotion programme whereby primary care is encouraged to continue offering a health education package.

The Association of Facilitators in Primary Care is a member organisation of the National Heart Forum.

References

1   Prochaska J, DiClemente C. 1986. *The Transtheoretical Approach: Crossing Traditional Boundaries of Therapy.* Homewood, Illinois: Dow Jones Irwin.

2   Office of Population Censuses and Surveys. 1991. *Classification of Occupations.* London: HMSO.

3   Hasley JC. 1994. *The Primary Health Care Team.* London: Royal Society of Medicine Press.

4   Department of Health. 1989. *Terms of Service for Doctors in General Practice.* London: HMSO.

5   Department of Health. 1993. *GP contract health promotion package: Guidance on implementation.* FHSL (93) 3. National Health Service Management Executive.

6   Simmonds O. 1994. *Social Variations in Coronary Heart Disease: Possibilities for Action. Report of a One-day Conference organised by the National Forum for Coronary Heart Disease Prevention.* (Unpublished).

Response to the OXCHECK Study and the British Family Heart Study

Public Health Network

The conclusions of the British Family Heart Study and the OXCHECK Study do not bear close relation to the findings. On a population basis, even if the benefits had been considerably less than those that were demonstrated, they would have been benefits worth having.

The studies focus only on the contribution from primary care. They take little or no account of the wider context and other actions or changes that may have been occurring in the wider community, such as messages in the media, that may also have been effecting a change in lifestyle. The Public Health Network supports the view expressed in a letter to the *British Medical Journal*[1] that there are different approaches to health promotion, which are complementary. These studies look at only one aspect of the totality; they do not take account of the fact that the effects of different interventions may be additive or even synergistic. Health promotion in general practice needs to be seen in the wider context as contributing to the overall strategy.

Both studies handed the responsibility for the interventions over to nurses. In the British Family Heart Study these were research nurses employed specifically for the study and in the OXCHECK Study they were the practice nurses. However, both give the impression of being 'bolt on' activities. From practical experience, the Public Health Network does not believe it would be possible to sustain the intensity of intervention in day-to-day primary care practice and suggests that further research is required using more realistic models involving other primary care staff. The potential of interactive computer technology in this field should also be explored.

Both studies attempt to change a number of risk factors such as smoking, weight, cholesterol levels and blood pressure. A hierarchy of

* The Public Health Network is a group of professionals involved in health promotion. It was established by the Department of Health.

factors was given in the OXCHECK Study although the details were not available. However, there is a danger that the studies attempted to change too many factors at the same time and that there would be greater success if fewer changes were attempted simultaneously. For example, there is already evidence of the effectiveness of GPs in reducing smoking.[2]

The studies demonstrated benefits across all grades of risk. However, these benefits are small for individuals at low risk and need to be weighed up against alternative ways of organising health promotion in primary care, for example by making more use of graded advice for a graded risk.

These studies look at only one year of follow-up. Although there is a rapid pay-off for many other interventions in primary care, the Public Health Network does not feel that follow-up has been long enough for this type of activity and believes that longer and more sustained effort will be required to demonstrate its full potential.

It is accepted that data will need to be collected from primary care to monitor health promotion activities. The current system appears to be over-inclusive and has overburdened practitioners in its collection. It would be better to request a smaller number of items and insist on higher quality data.

Conclusions

- The Public Health Network believes that the British Family Heart Study and the OXCHECK Study make a useful contribution to knowledge about CHD prevention but do not in themselves demonstrate that health promotion in primary care should be abandoned.

- There is an urgent need to understand what interventions are effective in reducing CHD risk. There is a need to understand which population groups should be targeted and by whom the intervention should be undertaken - for example by doctor, nurse or paramedic. Further research is required using more sophisticated and realistic models which take account of the wider context.

- There is a need for further training to enable clinicians to acquire skills in communicating health promotion messages and in understanding the population perspectives of this work. This training should begin in the undergraduate curriculum and continue throughout professional life.

- Interactive computer technology has the potential to play a role in this field and research is required to ensure that its potential is fully exploited.

This response was prepared on behalf of the Public Health Network by its Health Promotion Subgroup.

References

1 Pharoah P, Sanderson S. 1994. Health promotion contributes to the battle against heart disease. *British Medical Journal*; 308: 852.
2 Russell MAH, Wilson C, Baker CD. 1979. Effect of general practitioners' advice against smoking. *British Medical Journal*; 2: 231-235.

Response to the OXCHECK Study and the British Regional Heart Study

Comments from the OXCHECK Team

The general response of the OXCHECK Team to the critiques is to agree with most of them. However, some of the comments made reflect the unduly negative interpretation of the one-year results made by some, particularly by the media.[1]

As stated in the report of one-year follow-up results,[2] "the most convincing effect of health checks is the difference in cholesterol concentration between intervention and control groups ... the importance to public health of the observed effect on cholesterol concentration will be more easily assessed when the extent to which this effect is sustained is known". The conclusion that "we believe that final judgement on the value of health checks should at least await our three year results" was, of course, largely ignored. Now is the opportunity to make that judgement.

It is important to emphasise that the issue under consideration is the specific issue of the effectiveness of nurse-conducted health checks. These developed as a feature of general practice in the 1980s and became a contractual obligation for GPs in 1990. The question is whether they are effective, not whether they are more, or less, effective than other approaches to health promotion. There is widespread agreement that political, social, economic, and even legislative measures, as well as public health and community strategies and the influence of the media, all have major roles in determining the health of the nation. Any primary care initiatives can only be supplementary and complementary to these. But primary care is seen as a key medium for prevention and health promotion. The comprehensive coverage of the population by NHS general practice, and the reliability and credibility attributed to it by patients, endorse this role. Furthermore, prevention and health promotion have, since 1990, become part of the terms of service of GPs in the NHS.

There is, firstly, the issue of the outcome measures for health promotion. Very properly, both the OXCHECK Study and the British Family Heart Study were criticised not only for looking for physiological and bio-chemical measures of behaviour change but also for looking for quick changes - or short-term outcome measures. But the three-year results of the OXCHECK Study provide encouraging evidence of sustained, though modest, behavioural changes.

Criticism of the OXCHECK Study for focussing on risk factors, as opposed to health beliefs or state of well-being, is unjustified in the light of the initial aim. This was simply to examine the measurable parameters which could be subject to scientific scrutiny. This is the overwhelming strength of the OXCHECK Study approach.

Other criticisms were that the interventions were entirely nurse-led and with nurses working in isolation, with little evidence of direct GP involvement (except that GPs were already screening for and treating high blood pressure) or of practice teamwork: that the intervention was 'bolt on'. These comments are at least partially justified. But there is evidence that, in many general practices, doctor involvement in health promotion and teamwork are generally more limited than is often realised, so in this respect the OXCHECK Study may not be far removed from 'real life'. At least the health checks themselves had the quality of Rolls Royces rather than Minis.

The criticism that attempts to change too many factors at once are over-ambitious is justified. Audio-tape analysis of the 'content' of health checks indicates that smoking generally received less attention than diet. Other evidence suggests that smoking cessation may be better tackled on a separate occasion rather than as part of a health check. For many people, smoking is an addiction, not just a behaviour.

The criticism that there was no local community action or public health campaign to match the practice activity is also justified. But that is what happens in 'real life'.

It is important to acknowledge that the results of the OXCHECK Study *have* demonstrated a useful effect of nurse-conducted health checks on cardiovascular risk.[3] Better methods of doing health checks might produce better results. Although a patient-centred approach to lifestyle counselling was adopted, there is still much to learn about how best to help people to change. Acquiring the skills to effectively promote health is important.

The cost-effectiveness of such a programme must be carefully assessed, especially in the light of the expanding need for health care resources and their limited availability. The workload implications moreover are, of course, a major concern for primary care teams.

These comments were prepared on behalf of the OXCHECK Team by Dr Godfrey Fowler of the Imperial Cancer Research Fund General Practice Research Group, Department of Public Health and Primary Care, University of Oxford, with acknowledgements to Dr John Muir for his contribution to this paper and for his major role in the research.

Dr Fowler is an individual member of the National Heart Forum.

References

1   *Daily Telegraph.* July 19, 1993. GPs' £200m health drive 'is a flop'.
2   Imperial Cancer Research Fund OXCHECK Study Group. 1994. Effectiveness of health checks conducted by nurses in primary care: results of OXCHECK Study after one year. *British Medical Journal*; 308: 308-312.
3   Imperial Cancer Research Fund OXCHECK Study Group. 1995. Effectiveness of health checks conducted by nurses in primary care: final results of the OXCHECK Study. *British Medical Journal*; 310: 1099-1104.

Response to the OXCHECK Study and the British Family Heart Study

Comments from the British Family Heart Study Group

When a person is invited to participate in a cardiovascular screening and intervention programme, he or she might reasonably ask three questions:

- Will I feel any better?
- Will my risk of coronary disease be reduced and, if so, by how much and over what period of time?
- Will I live longer?

The British Family Heart Study was undertaken to evaluate the effectiveness of a nurse-led cardiovascular screening programme in primary care, by determining whether such an intervention could reduce coronary risk factors over one year. The national trial was planned during 1988 and, following the appointments of the nurse and medical coordinators, a pilot study was conducted in 1989 at Aldermoor Health Centre in Southampton. The main study, completed by 26 general practices in 13 towns, started in January 1990 before the government's new health checks (with a reimbursement of £40 for 10 patients seen in not less than an hour) were introduced.

The study was innovative in several important respects:
1 A population approach to prevention was adopted by offering systematic screening to all adults (40-59 years), given that most coronary events occur outside high-risk groups.
2 Primary care was chosen as the most appropriate setting for a systematic population-based cardiovascular screening and lifestyle intervention programme, led by specially trained nurses, even though systematic screening was not the traditional way general practice works.

3   Families rather than patients were targeted because it was believed that lifestyle intervention in relation to smoking, eating habits and physical activity was more effective if the whole family was involved.

4   A coronary risk score was used, summarising the combined impact of risk factors, to estimate for a man, or woman, the risk of developing coronary disease relative to a man or woman of the same age. There was thus a departure from the traditional medical screening model in which patients are classified as 'normal' or not. The word 'normal' was erased from the nurses' vocabulary and instead, the men or women in the study were given their overall coronary risk and this determined the intensity of lifestyle intervention.

5   The nurses did not simply give advice and hand out health education leaflets. They were specially trained in a patient-centred approach to change. Appointments of nurses were made locally by the practice team in consultation with the nurse coordinator. Nurses spent their first week in the practice familiarising themselves with the staff and the surgery and then had a week of training. This training used a learner-centred approach: each session began with both the group and tutors defining their needs. At the end of the session participants reviewed the extent to which these needs were met. They learnt how to integrate patient-centred consulting on behaviour change with risk assessment and use of the study protocols for recall and referral, and of the patient-held booklet *Your Passport to Health*. This educational model was then used in turn by the nurses for the family-centred intervention programme.

The nurses then returned to the practice for six weeks and started the programme by screening and providing health promotion for families. They then had a further three days of training to reflect on and share their initial experiences, and develop their understanding of this approach to health promotion. Three further single review days were held over 18 months to review progress and reinforce the approach. The nurses were not 'deposited within surgeries' as suggested in the response of the Association of Facilitators in Primary Care, or 'bolted on' like a portacabin extension to the premises.

Although the object of the British Family Heart Study programme was lifestyle change - smoking, diet and physical activity - the principal outcome measures were risk factors rather than behaviour change. This was for one principal reason. The complexity of measuring for example diet, to obtain valid and reproducible estimates for individuals or groups is considerable, and the *practical* and *financial* implications of measuring behavioural change greatly exceeded the hard won resources available for the trial. However, attenders' perceptions of their risks of heart disease prior to screening were documented and, at the time of printing this report, were being analysed to find out how they affected attenders' subsequent outcome, and their perceptions of their ability to improve their risk status. This point must be emphasised because some of the responses, while drawing attention to the desirability of measuring behavioural change, take little or no account of the complexities of conducting a randomised controlled trial in the free-living population.

Professor McPherson's paper (see page 27) outlines the paradigm of the randomised controlled trial through which evidence is now gathered, and by which its conclusiveness and relevance are judged, and expresses concern about this model being the sole arbiter of scientific evidence.

The randomised controlled trial as an experimental model originated in agricultural research and becomes less robust as the research moves from fields of wheat to populations of people. Classically, in a randomised experiment in the laboratory all factors are held constant, except for the factor of experimental interest, which is then varied and its effect measured. It is possible to conclude from such an experiment (allowing for the play of chance) that any change was a consequence of varying the experimental factor and nothing else. Such an experiment estimates the true effect of an intervention.

When this experimental model is applied to a free-living population where individuals, or indeed whole communities, are randomised to treatment or control, the effect measured is that which can be achieved in the real world. The threat to the experimental design comes from the possibility of the randomisation breaking down, due to drop-outs from one arm of the study being different from the other. The threat to the intervention evaluation comes from possible health-related changes in society which may reduce any treatment difference between the two arms of a study.

However, if the design is robust, such a pragmatic trial gives an estimate of the impact of a specified intervention which is feasible in a particular setting, taking into account the variable behaviour of both those offering the intervention, and those taking it up. Such studies are analysed properly by 'intention to treat' in order to respect the random allocation of individuals, irrespective of their actual behaviour in the two arms. Estimates of treatment effect are thus always smaller in such a study than the intervention is capable of achieving under ideal conditions.

However, where this model can be applied and the result appropriately interpreted, this experimental approach has a potent contribution to make to evidence-based practice.

Interpretation of the principal results of the study

It has been estimated that the British Family Heart Study intervention led to a 12% (statistically significant) reduction in coronary risk (that is the risk of developing a non-fatal myocardial infarction or dying from coronary disease over 10 years) in the intervention group at one year. This risk reduction was similar in men and women. In interpreting this result the British Family Heart Study Group did not say, as some of the responses suggest, that "health promotion in primary care should be abandoned". The Group said: "the (government's) new health promotion package cannot be justified in its present form from the results of this trial".

Nor did the Group "blame the nurses" as some critics appear to believe; the nurses and their colleagues in the general practices in the British Family Heart Study were held in the very highest regard. The source of that criticism seems to be the Department of Health's comment following the publication of the results of the study: "The findings ... do show that using a nurse in a clinic setting with no GP involvement is not an effective way of organising health promotion."[1]

The British Family Heart Study Group took the view that the government's current health promotion package could not be justified because the Group believes that the nature and intensity of the family-based screening and intervention programme, led by specially trained nurses, was likely to exceed the efforts of all but the most devoted and well resourced of general practices and therefore the reduction in coronary risk in the generality of practices as a result of current initiatives is likely to be smaller than 12%, if indeed there is any reduction in risk at all.

It is particularly important to appreciate in this respect that the government's current arrangement offers financial reimbursement primarily for screening (collecting data) and not for the quality of intervention and follow-up. For those who argue that a 12% reduction in coronary risk is worthwhile, and this is a matter of judgement, and would like to achieve this by implementing a family-based programme, it is estimated that for a practice with a list size of 1,000 men (40-59 years) at least four full-time nurses would be needed to screen and intervene over 18 months in these men and their partners. This, of course, greatly exceeds the resources currently available for health promotion for any one general practice.

How big does an effect have to be to be worthwhile? As the Public Health Network claimed: "on a population basis, even if the benefits had been considerably less than those that were demonstrated, they would have been benefits worth having." But is this true?

To answer this question, it is first necessary to establish what is meant by an estimated 12% reduction in coronary risk. The absolute risk of developing coronary disease was calculated using the Dundee risk score for the intervention and comparison groups. The relative (or percentage) difference between these two risks is estimated at 12%, that is a 12% reduction in risk in the intervention group compared to the comparison group. If the screening and intervention programme used in this trial were implemented in the same way by every general practice in the country, and if such programmes achieved the same reductions in risk factors which were then maintained in the long term, is this 12% reduction big enough to be worthwhile in terms of the public health?

To answer that question it is important to establish how big is the absolute risk of developing coronary disease in this country to which this percentage risk reduction will apply. The answer from the 1994 WHO MONICA data[2] is that the absolute risk of developing and dying from coronary disease in the UK is bigger than almost anywhere else in the world. So is not any reduction, of any size, worthwhile given the high absolute risk in the UK population?

This will depend on the proportion of the population to which the risk reduction (whatever size it is) would apply. For example, a risk reduction of 50% applied to 0.001% of the population would have no appreciable public health impact, whereas a risk reduction of 5% applied to the whole population would have, relatively speaking, a much greater impact. So to whom will the 12% risk reduction found in the British Family Heart Study apply?

The answer to this question needs to take account of the initial non-response to the invitation to screening and those who dropped out of the screening programme over one year. With a response rate of 73% and a non-return rate of up to 15% at one year, the population to whom this risk reduction could apply is over half of all adults in the middle years of life, although after the first year this number will continue to diminish with further losses to the programme. Even so, this programme reached a majority of the adult population.

Another factor which must be taken into account is the cost: staff (nursing, medical and other health professionals such as nutritionists), staff training, screening equipment, resources for health promotion and drugs. Put crudely, if a 12% reduction in risk over one year, by two-thirds of the adult population cost the government all its gold reserves, would it be justified? The answer is, of course, yes or no, depending on one's point of view. In other words it is a judgement, and final judgement should be reserved until the results of the cost-effectiveness analyses of both the British Family Heart Study and the OXCHECK Study have been reviewed.

For the present there is evidence that a systematic, population-based cardiovascular screening programme, led by full-time specially trained nurses working with the practice team, and using a family-centred lifestyle intervention programme, can reduce the risk of developing CHD by about 12% among participants after one year. If this programme were to be developed in the same way in every practice in the country, with the considerable resource implications already described, it could reach about two-thirds of the population. When this scenario is contrasted with the new health promotion package with financial remuneration based on data collection rather than on intervention and follow-up, it becomes clear why the utility of the government's programme must remain in considerable doubt, and why the British Family Heart Study Group believes the programme cannot be justified in its present form by the results of these trials.

Implications

Some key issues in terms of research and policy in relation to cardiovascular screening and health promotion in general practice must be addressed.

Research

The British Family Heart Study Group agrees with the views advanced by Professor McPherson (see page 27) in relation to the interpretation of preventive interventions and accept his view that in establishing the attributable effect of multifactorial interventions almost everything is attenuated by the complicated processes involved in the mechanisms required to make such a programme work. These programmes are likely to be influenced by the readiness of individuals to change (or not); the learning curve of health professionals and the population; the real difficulties of achieving lifestyle changes; the appropriateness (or not) of trying to modify several risk factors simultaneously; the length of time over which such interventions may be seen to be beneficial (or not); the complexities of measuring lifestyle; and of course the public health context in which such screening and health promotion is offered.

All of these factors do not necessarily fit comfortably with the rigours of a randomised controlled trial design, which is the sole basis of the current evaluation, but they all need to be investigated. Good quality research is needed to develop and evaluate new approaches to prevention. Without research it is not possible to know how effective one strategy is compared to another and therefore how much more needs to be done to prevent this disease. Such research should inform policy.

Policy
The present policy on health promotion only monitors risk factor data collection in general practice, the outcome of which in terms of health gain is simply not known. This emphasis on data collection is widely perceived by many GPs, and other health professionals, as valueless. This unfocused activity may detract from other more productive roles for health professionals in prevention.

The results of the British Family Heart Study provide the Department of Health, in consultation with other professional groups, with an important opportunity to change the priorities and content of their present policy. The British Family Heart Study Group argues for a more selective approach to preventive medicine making patients with CHD, and other vascular diseases, the top priority - Band 1. Band 2 would include other high-risk individuals identified in clinical practice, for example those with hypertension, hyperlipidaemia or diabetes and the families of these patients. The rest of the population would constitute Band 3.

Within this order of priorities it is important to identify these patients and assess their coronary risk, but there should also be a commitment to intervention and follow-up and to audit of the effectiveness of professional activity. Until the health care team can demonstrate effective care for those with established coronary disease, or other diseases which increase the risk of developing coronary disease, there can be little justification for spreading preventive efforts more widely. There is an important opportunity here for the Department of Health to capitalise on the flexibility of the banding system to provide financial reward for those practices applying a rational risk-related strategy, including resources for intervention and follow-up, rather than for returning screening figures alone. Wherever new approaches to prevention are advocated, these trials emphasise the need for, and show the feasibility (against all the odds) of, rigorous scientific evaluation to measure the impact of such strategies in clinical practice.

Public health policy
Finally, the British Family Heart Study Group supports the views expressed by several contributors that there are different approaches to health promotion of which cardiovascular screening and lifestyle intervention in primary care is only one. As the Study Group clearly stated in its paper, " ... primary care alone cannot provide a population approach to reducing cardiovascular risk and the government in aiming to reduce the prevalence of risk factors will also need to put in place more effective public health policies on tobacco control and healthy eating".

Tobacco consumption is a very good example of the importance of the public health context and the hypocrisy of a government which is not prepared to tackle the tobacco industry, for example by banning tobacco advertising, but makes smoking the Band 1 priority of the health promotion contract, a priority which remains in place despite the depressing evidence from trials of a failure to favourably modify smoking habits in the adult population by this approach.

Public health initiatives in relation to tobacco consumption, healthy eating, and physical activity may be a great deal more important in relation to reducing the burden of this disease in this country than any contribution made from primary care cardiovascular screening programmes.

These comments were prepared on behalf of the British Family Heart Study Group by Professor David Wood, of the Department of Clinical Epidemiology, National Heart and Lung Institute, and Professor Ann-Louise Kinmonth of the Primary Medical Care Group, University of Southampton. Professor Wood represents the British Cardiac Society on the National Heart Forum.

References
1   Verified by personal communication between the Department of Health and R Leyden, August 1995.

2   Tunstall-Pedoe H, Kuulasmaa K, Amouyel P, Arveiler D, Rajakangas AM, Pajak A. 1994. Myocardial infarction and coronary deaths in the World Health Organization MONICA Project. Registration procedures, event rates, and case-fatality rates in 38 populations from 21 countries in four continents. *Circulation*; 90; 1: 583-612.

Response to the OXCHECK Study and the British Family Heart Study

Discussion

The following is a summary of the discussion held at the expert meeting.

Both the OXCHECK Study and the British Family Heart Study led to impressive reductions in serum cholesterol levels in men and women. Although there were reductions in blood pressure, these may have been influenced by accommodation. There were no substantial reductions in smoking prevalence.

Before drawing firm conclusions about the studies, there needs to be an economic evaluation of each intervention, and an examination of the extent to which the changes in risk factors can be maintained in the long term, and what sort of input would be needed to maintain them. (The final results of the OXCHECK Study, however, show that it is possible to maintain change.[1])

Both studies were designed to find out if it is possible to change risk factors through interventions within primary care. They indicate that such interventions can produce modest but worthwhile results.

It is now important to examine other strategies for interventions in primary care - for example whether there would be a greater effect on risk factor changes if the whole primary health care team were involved in the intervention rather than just the practice nurse, or if the intervention tackled single risk factors rather than multiple risk factors. It is also necessary to look at how the results of the two studies can be used in practice.

Epidemiology

The British Family Heart Study found an estimated 12% reduction in coronary risk (the risk of developing a non-fatal myocardial infarction or dying from coronary disease over 10 years) in the intervention group at one year, based on the changes in risk factors. If this level of intervention were implemented by every practice in the country, it could translate into an 8% reduction in non-fatal myocardial infarction and coronary deaths.

This calculation assumes that changes in risk factors will bring about changes in CHD morbidity and mortality. There is overwhelming evidence that cholesterol, blood pressure and smoking are causally related to cardiovascular disease, including CHD. However, population intervention studies have not always brought about reductions in CHD. Although in the WHO Study, a lowering of risk factors resulted in a reduction in CHD incidence and mortality, other intervention studies including MRFIT, the Gothenburg study and the Helsinki study, did not result in such a reduction. The North Karelia study showed dramatic reductions in risk factors and a reduction in CHD incidence and mortality but reductions in CHD also happened in other parts of Finland at the time of the study. It is important to investigate the reasons why some intervention studies do not find an effect on CHD incidence and mortality. This may be due to the design of individual studies, or there may be contamination from the intervention group to the control group, or problems with interpretation of the results.

The question is not whether changes in risk factors lead to changes in disease patterns, but what is the impact of interventions: can risk factors be changed by interventions in primary care? The UK primary care system might offer greater potential for change than, for example, interventions in factories.

More research is also needed to find out more about the risk factors that are important in the groups currently thought to be at low risk. Psychosocial factors, antioxidants, and insulin resistance may all play a part.

Where do we go from here?

Future structure and financing of primary care
If primary care is to offer an integrated service for patients, offering a population approach to CHD prevention, there needs to be a radical restructuring of the way in which primary care is currently financed and resourced. Primary care has an important role in prevention, but it needs appropriate facilities and resources in order to carry out that role effectively. The question of whether primary care should be GP-led is still a subject of debate.

A high-risk approach or a population approach?
Both the OXCHECK Study and the British Family Heart Study showed modest but real changes in risk factors across the whole distribution, not simply at the top end of the risk curve. However, the greatest changes were observed in the high-risk groups, who also received the most intense interventions. Other studies have also indicated that interventions can produce greater benefit among high-risk than among low-risk groups.

There is evidence that the current management of high-risk patients - for example those with ischaemic heart disease, hypertension, atrial fibrillation, or chronic heart failure - is not particularly good, and that there is much scope for improvement. Primary health care teams have a responsibility to look after those people well first before dealing with other lower risk groups. In the light of this, and given the stronger evidence of effectiveness of health promotion interventions in high-risk compared to low-risk groups, there is a strong case for primary care teams to make high-risk patients a priority group.

There is a finite amount of resources - both time and money - for CHD prevention activity. If primary care teams are asked to do more to deal with high-risk people, either more funding has to be provided, or the banding system has to be altered, for example by reducing the age range of people seen, or by seeing people less frequently. If primary care is to become a 'franchise' responsible for delivering NHS screening, then much clearer policy guidance is needed both on the content of the screening and the target groups.

Cholesterol
One of the most noticeable changes in risk factors in the OXCHECK Study and British Family Heart Study was the reduction in cholesterol levels. The British Family Heart Study did attempt to investigate the effect of cholesterol testing versus no cholesterol testing, to find out whether testing specifically made any contribution to the overall reduction of risk, but was unable to answer the question. Further research is needed to find out to what extent cholesterol testing itself stimulates behaviour change and contributes to a reduction in cholesterol levels.

Should the government's health promotion programme be adapted?
GPs can currently choose one of three bands in the health promotion banding system. Each band requires a different level of data collection and intervention (see Appendix 1). While there is scope for flexibility

within the current arrangements,* the financial rewards for GPs depend on the level of data collection rather than on the quality of the intervention or amount of follow-up.

Data collection has three purposes:
1 Data on a specific general practice can be used to inform the activities of individual primary health care teams.
2 The data collected by GPs can be aggregated and used to inform public health policy.
3 Health authorities can use the data for monitoring purposes to ensure accountability.

There is much scepticism among primary health care team members about the need for data collection, partly due to the fact that it is the collection of data rather than the quality of health promotion pro-grammes that currently determines the financial reimbursement to GPs. A more positive view of data collection could be achieved by:
- offering primary health care teams training in how they can use the data to inform their practice
- demonstrating to teams the value of their data for local needs assess-ment and to inform public health policy, and
- emphasising that the health promotion banding system offers primary care teams scope for flexibility.*

The amount of information that GPs are required to collect should be reduced, and more emphasis should be placed on the quality of interventions. Follow-up of patients is essential.

A broader definition of health promotion?
Health promotion is increasingly equated with changing measurable risk factors among individuals. It is important to undertake broader health promotion measures, including policy interventions, to tackle eating habits and smoking behaviour among school children, for example.

Conclusion

The OXCHECK Study and the British Family Heart Study were designed to examine whether it is possible to change risk factors

---

* *Paragraph 30, Schedule 3 of the GPs' terms of service (Health Promotion Band 3) requires GPs to: "ascertain relevant information on the target population at appropriate levels of coverage and in the light of this carry out a programme of lifestyle interventions for those found to be at risk of CHD/ stroke, concentrating on priority groups within the target population".*

through interventions in primary care. Both interventions produced small but worthwhile changes in risk factors in the short term. Before a final judgement can be made about the way forward, there must be a close examination of the economic evaluation of the interventions, and of whether the changes are sustained in the long term.

Given the finite resources for primary care, there are strong arguments for adopting a high-risk approach to CHD prevention: such an approach yields better results, and there is much scope for improving current management of high-risk patients.

The OXCHECK Study and the British Family Heart Study tested only certain strategies; there may be other, better ways of achieving reductions in risk factors in primary care. CHD is a major chronic disease in the UK, and there are clearly opportunities for health promotion which need to be investigated. The possibilities are significant.

References

1   Imperial Cancer Research Fund OXCHECK Study Group. 1995. Effectiveness of health checks conducted by nurses in primary care: final results of the OXCHECK Study. *British Medical Journal*; 310: 1099-1104.

Chapter 5

Implications

This chapter outlines the implications for practice, policy and research. It is based on the workshops and discussions at the expert meeting.

Implications for practice

Key lessons from the two studies

The primary health care team has an important role in health promotion. The role of each individual needs to be integrated via practice protocols and policies. Practice nurses need to be supported by training and motivation through performance appraisal.

Behaviour change is complex and takes a long time, and appropriate outcome measures need to be used for evaluation and monitoring of health promotion interventions. Health professionals need to have realistic expectations of the extent of change that is possible. GPs and nurses can be demotivated by small changes at an individual or practice level, even though they may be contributing important changes at a population level.

There are still areas of uncertainty concerning the effectiveness of health promotion within primary care. Further research is required to evaluate a range of different approaches, particularly in terms of the length of time spent on the health check. The effectiveness of the 'family intervention' approach can be considered when the findings of the British Family Heart Study on this issue are published. Clarification of the issue of cholesterol management at research, policy and practice level is also needed.

When the results of research are published, it is important to take proactive steps to counteract potential adverse press coverage. Also, it may be better to limit the number of messages conveyed from each study so that health practitioners are not overwhelmed with too much information.

Skills and systems for information management need to be developed locally and nationally. The NHS Executive needs to have a sound mechanism for accountability. The data collection for health promotion banding should be geared towards assessing the needs of the population.

Financial incentives to individual GPs for health promotion (1990 GP contract) do not necessarily encourage a team or population approach.

Primary health care can play only one part in the primary prevention of coronary heart disease (CHD). Since a single general practice could not possibly provide primary prevention to all the necessary people, clear priorities need to be set, any necessary restructuring carried out, and appropriate resources allocated.

Recommendations

The role of the primary health care team and practice development
- **Each practice needs to determine its readiness for change and identify the barriers to change.** This process may be assisted by a facilitator.

- **Each practice needs to develop a health promotion strategy.** This should clearly specify what it is attempting to achieve. The strategy should be agreed and understood by all members of the practice.

- **Effective teamworking needs to be encouraged and supported.** The expertise and potential role of each primary care team member in health promotion needs to be recognised and used appropriately. It is also important to address the issues which can pose barriers to teamworking, for example turnover of staff, and the fact that team members report to different managers. Also, practice teams are being approached by an increasing number of specialists - such as different types of facilitator, and community nurse managers. This is beginning to pose problems since many practices do not have either the time or resources to act on their offers of help.

- **One person should take 'lead' responsibility for the practice's health promotion activities.** That person should have a remit to ensure that there is adequate and appropriate health promotion training and allowance for protected time. This responsibility needs to be agreed by all decision-makers in the practice.

Education and training in health promotion
- **There should be an obligation for all primary health care team members involved in health promotion to have a certain level of training, with minimum requirements, before undertaking health**

promotion work. The Family Health Services Authority (FHSA) could play a role in monitoring by setting minimum training levels as a criterion for acceptance for health promotion banding.

- **The teaching of health promotion and disease prevention needs to be included in the basic education of all health professionals.** This teaching needs to be integrated within post-basic (vocational and higher professional) training, and included in continuing education. Teaching should include behaviour change and communication skills to convey clear messages to patients.

- **Multidisciplinary training on health promotion should be encouraged.** Training should acknowledge that health professionals have differing roles and spend different amounts of time with patients.

- **Clear and effective models of intervention, which have universal consensus, need to be agreed as the basis for standard practice, and incorporated within the education and training of health professionals.** As more effective interventions are developed, training should be updated accordingly.

- **Mentoring from other practices (observing good models of practice) should be used in the training of primary health care professionals.**

- **The expertise within various disciplines needs to be acknowledged for provision of training.**

Provision and quality of care

- **Practices need to establish which are their priority, high-risk groups and develop strategies for reaching them.** Practices also need to ensure that there is a proper mechanism for dealing with low-risk and medium-risk groups via an agreed practice protocol.

- **There needs to be clarification of the division of responsibility between GPs and hospital doctors during the period immediately after patients leave hospital.** There is a need for better coordination, particularly in terms of lifestyle advice offered to patients during this period.

- **Health professionals need to listen to and acknowledge the concerns of patients.** If their concerns are not acknowledged, this leads to dissatisfaction and poor adherence to health promotion advice.

- **Health promotion advice to patients should concentrate on a few simple messages.** Primary care professionals are more likely to offer patients advice on cardiovascular health promotion if they have a few simple messages which they can reasonably easily implement within their practice, and which all members of the team believe in.

- **Primary health care teams should direct some of their health promotion advice to under 16s.** Many young people start smoking at the age of 12-13.

Data collection and audit
- **Standard definitions for the measurement and recording of risk factors need to be developed.** In particular, the recording and management of blood pressure need to be standardised.

- **Practices should make greater use of the data collected.** Data could be used for prioritising activity within the practice, and for audit purposes to monitor activities and improve services offered by the practice.

- **Data should be aggregated and used, along with community profiles, for local needs assessment and to inform the development of local strategies.** Differences between urban and rural areas, and ethnic and social class variations, need to be considered.

Building health alliances
- **General practices need to work closely with public health, health promotion, community nursing, local hospitals and trusts and FHSAs in developing strategies on a locality basis.** These locality approaches need to be considered in purchasing. Models have been developed across the country that could provide guidance.

- **The role of primary health care in the prevention of CHD needs to be part of a national, integrated strategy.**

Resources and funding for health promotion
- **A substantial injection of resources for health promotion is needed.** Resources are needed for the development of health promotion activities, information technology, manpower and education and training.

- **GPs need to be involved with health authority purchasing to influence the transfer of funds from secondary to primary health care.**

This section is based largely on the reports of two expert meeting workshops on Implications for practice. *The workshops were chaired by Dr Tony Dowell and Janet Bailey, with reports written by Lisa Bullard-Cawthorne and Amanda Killoran.*

Implications for policy

Key lessons from the two studies

The OXCHECK Study and the British Family Heart Study suggest that a significant effect could be obtained in primary care, but this requires a co-ordinated approach.

Both studies focussed on specific measurements over a short timescale. It is too soon to assess the long-term effects on cardiovascular prevention.

The studies demonstrated what could be done by practices with additional resources rather than by practices with current levels of resources. Neither study assessed the likely impact on the communities involved.

Environmental context and constraints

National

The conflicting policies of government create problems for primary health care teams. For example, it is difficult to reconcile the *Health of the Nation* strategy and the GP contract with the absence of a ban on tobacco advertising.

Commissioning

There is a need to balance the priorities identified in primary health care with those identified by health commissions.

Health authorities have been slow to change contracts and to support initiatives in primary care. Contracts reflect historic practice rather than a move towards health promotion and outcomes.

There is currently no minimum specified amount that health authorities have to spend on health promotion. For health promotion to flourish, there needs to be a real shift of resources. A start has been made in Wales where, in 1995-96, 0.75% of health authorities' revenue budget was allocated to health education and promotion.

The focus on needs assessment and designing programmes to meet identified needs seems to have weakened. Use of tools such as the Community Oriented Primary Care programme could help this process.

Primary health care

Terms such as 'health promotion' and 'primary care' need to be carefully defined.

The current direction of health care policy is towards a primary care led NHS, with organisations of 40-50 people, yet the literature and studies largely focus on primary health care teams of 8-10 people.

Primary care is bombarded by competing agendas: for example mental health, incontinence etc. Cardiovascular prevention is part of the widening agenda for primary care. It should be seen in the context of developing organisations which have the capability, and capacity, to look to the future.

The individuals who make up primary health care organisations may have as many as six different employers. Problems are further compounded by the staff turnover, particularly in cities.

Health promotion

Health professionals currently have difficulty in adapting their practice as the health promotion messages change.

Health professionals have little training in methods of helping people to change their behaviour.

Recommendations

Health promotion is an essential part of primary care. The OXCHECK Study and the British Family Heart Study indicate that health promotion activities should continue, but that it should be adapted in the light of both the research and feedback from practitioners. A move to evidence-based practice should be supported.

National
- **The conflicting government policies which impact on health should be reconciled.**

- **There is a need for explicit professional consensus about health promotion in primary care.** Efforts should be made to examine different models of delivering health promotion in a primary care setting. This should include dentists, pharmacists and opticians who are not well integrated into the scheme and who see different client groups.

- **It may be necessary to re-examine the age ranges and intensity of follow-up required by the health promotion banding system.** A more intensive intervention may be needed in order to improve quality.

- **There should be an explicit rationale for the coverage levels suggested by the Department of Health's health promotion programme.** There is as yet no evidence that 90% coverage of the practice population is the correct level at which to set policy.

Commissioning

- **Health promotion in primary care should be set in the context of an overall strategy for health promotion within districts.** The strategy should encompass groups (including some potentially high-risk groups) who are currently not presenting in primary care. Local programmes should be graded on the basis of need.

- **Innovative approaches to contracting should be tried through the local commissioning process.** Potential new entrants should include primary care organisations as well as traditional suppliers. There is a need for an integrated approach to commissioning, including closer links between public health, primary care, and health authority commissioners.

- **Consideration should be given to how primary care organisations can reach priority groups currently outside the banding system: for example under 16s.** Primary care should find ways of meeting the needs of those adolescents who do not visit their GP. School health policies are also important and should be considered and formulated.

- **Further consideration should be given to individuals with existing CHD.** These patients should be followed up, and the effectiveness of interventions should be assessed.

Evidence-based practice

- **Resources should be invested in interventions which have been shown to be effective.** For example, nicotine patches and gum should be available on prescription to selected groups.

- Fundholding and other investments may be able to support innovation in practice, but there is a need to monitor and evaluate experiments and new approaches before they are disseminated.

Monitoring and accountability
- While monitoring and accountability are both important, methods for accountability should allow for local flexibility. The monitoring mechanism should be through a contract with the organisation rather than with an individual practitioner, thus encouraging a team-based approach through accreditation of the organisation.
- There should be a shift in emphasis from coverage and data collection as the measure of performance, towards measurement of the quality of interventions. Clinical audit should be the vehicle for providing the incentive for action and for change in organisations.
- Work should be undertaken on confidentiality, and the rights of users who either do not wish to take part or do not want their data to be recorded. Protection for users should be built into any policy recommendations.

Definitions
- Given the changes in the organisation of primary care, there is a need for clear definitions of terminology. For example, terms such as primary care, primary health care, primary health care organisation, health promotion, and community need to be clearly defined.

Training and skills
- The undergraduate curriculum for all those entering the health professions should include training in health promotion. This includes the curricula for dentistry, pharmacy, nursing, medicine and the professions allied to medicine.
- Health professionals' knowledge of and skills in health promotion should be regularly updated. This can be done through postgraduate training and continuing professional development programmes.
- Training in health promotion should go beyond the traditional bio-medical model of health, to a more sociological model which embraces more fully the cognitive therapies.
- Health promotion training should be organised for multi-disciplinary as well as for single profession groups. This will help health professionals to gain a better understanding of each other's skills and roles.

- **Education packages should include support with information systems, and handling and interpretation of data.**

- **Health professionals should have more exposure to research methodologies.** This could be achieved both through education and practical application and would help to create a culture of enquiry and willingness to change.

Support
- **The strategy to deliver health promotion through primary care should be linked to the wider agenda of developing the organisational capacity of primary care.** Failure to do this will result in delivery of health promotion by the exceptional rather than the average organisation.

- **The role and functions of the public health discipline need to be re-assessed as an independent community resource accessible to primary care.** Primary health care teams need access to independent public health advice.

- **Medical Audit Advisory Groups (MAAGs), or their successors, should help facilitate development in primary care teams.** This could include organisational development.

- **Consideration should be given to inter-agency working on the ground.** For example, links between local organisations could be created, and community participation encouraged, as in the North Karelia project in Finland.

Data/intelligence
- **The amount of data to be collected by general practices should be reduced to a minimum.** The interim report and routine collection of data on body mass index should no longer be required. Data collected should be meaningful, manageable, easy to collect, pertinent to the person collecting it, valued by those using it, and compatible with other data sets.

- **Primary health care organisations should receive feedback on the data submitted.** This would help to create a positive spiral of performance review and feedback.

This section is based largely on the reports of two expert meeting workshops on Implications for policy. *The workshops were chaired by Dr Tim van Zwannenberg and Dr Viv Speller and reports were written by Chris Shearin and Aislinn O'Dwyer.*

Implications for research

Key lessons from the two studies

Both the OXCHECK Study and the British Family Heart Study led to declines in serum cholesterol in men and women. The OXCHECK Study showed that these declines were sustainable over three years. However, the interventions were unsuccessful in helping smokers to quit.

The research methodology did not take into account the readiness of patients to change their behaviour.

Both studies were resource-intensive in terms of time both for practice staff and patients. The results of the cost-benefit analyses from the two studies will be key to understanding the implications of the results.

Environmental context and constraints

The primary health care team operates in the context of changes in society as a whole as well as within the NHS and the team's locality. The constraints on the team act at many different levels.

National and societal

Levels of deprivation have increased in society over the 1980s and early 90s. This is one reason for a rise in demand for the services provided by GPs. The emphasis and priority which patients and service users can give to lifestyle changes has diminished with increasing deprivation.

The primary care team is one element in the total picture and cannot act in isolation from policies set at a national level, such as the regulation of food labelling and tobacco advertising.

The National Health Service and the primary health care team

The profile of services delivered by the primary health care team in a community setting has been raised, and expectations have increased substantially. At the same time, there is low morale in the primary care team and a feeling of being overloaded by 'top down' priorities and targets. There is a lack of ownership of these targets and of the data collected as a requirement of the GP contract. There is also some disillusionment with the outcomes of health promotion in primary care, although this is not shared by all public health professionals.

Teamwork and alliances
The importance of teamwork and team roles in primary care should be stressed. It is important to recognise the diversity of the primary care team and the need for closer links between public health professionals and the voluntary sector, and for the formation of health alliances.

Knowledge, attitudes and trends
There is uncertainty as to which health promotion interventions work. There is a need for better theoretical models, and/or a need for existing models to be better validated experimentally.

There is concern that GPs should not be seen as having the *prime* responsibility for health promotion in the general population.

It is important, however, to recognise and to build on the fact that some trends are moving in the right direction. Smoking rates are falling and many smokers have the advantage of having seen someone quit successfully.

The implications for research in primary care

Research methodologies
Limitations of the randomised control trial
The randomised control trial (RCT) is regarded as one of the most important methodologies in clinical research. However, RCTs are not the best way of evaluating health promotion interventions for the following reasons:

- *Lack of robustness*
Subjects in control groups may be exposed to the intervention. Unifactorial trials have often been successful but multifactorial trials have not, largely because of such contamination.

- *Difficulty in extrapolating results*
It is difficult to extrapolate the results of unifactorial trials with high-risk subjects to population programmes where the majority of subjects may be at low risk.

- *Contamination and confounding*

Contamination and confounding in trials can mean that the results are over-interpreted. The observed reductions in risk may apply not only to those in the intervention group but also to some of those in the control group.

- *Unrealistic interventions*

RCTs are often designed without practical considerations in mind. Ideal interventions in terms of clinical outcome may be unrealistic given resource constraints.

Some of these limitations may be overcome by improving the design of RCTs, for example by randomising practices and doctors rather than patients. In addition observational studies and studies employing qualitative methods could be run in tandem with RCTs to enable a better understanding of the intervention process. There may also be a need to combine elements from clinical and qualitative observational studies in a more effective way.

The role of behavioural research

The role of behavioural research in health promotion research was highlighted by both the OXCHECK Study and the British Family Heart Study. It appears that psychosocial (behavioural) research can inform intervention studies through:

- investigations of the barriers to and process of behavioural change
- refining methods of giving lifestyle advice and counselling, and
- developing appropriate psychological outcome criteria.

The population approach versus targeted interventions

The studies raise the question of how best to intervene in populations where the majority of people may be at medium and low risk. What priority should purchasers give to wider public health activities, such as encouraging regulation of food composition and food labelling, super-market layout, availability and access to cheap, nutritious foods, and tobacco control? Efforts at this level may have a greater effect on behaviour change in the population.*

Recommendations

General principles for the type of research needed and the methodologies developed were identified, as well as specific areas where research is needed.

---

* Long-running intervention studies, such as the North Karelia study or the Australian melanoma programme, have not been able to assess the relative roles of primary care, public broadcasting campaigns and other population strategies.

General principles: a checklist for research funders and researchers

- **Research funding bodies should ensure that all new large-scale trials include a systematic review of previous studies if one has not already been carried out.** A systematic review, which should cover both published and unpublished studies, is vital for helping to define and refine research questions.

- **Research questions in health promotion need to be defined more clearly.** Researchers need to make explicit, before the study starts, what would constitute a 'clinically significant' outcome.

- **The views of consumers and users of services should be given more prominence.** Consumers should play a greater role in deciding which trials to fund and which methodologies to use.

- **RCTs and observational studies should be combined or carried out in tandem to tease out the important elements in the intervention process.** For example, it is important to find out how patients react to different members of the primary health care team, as well as the effect of different interventions.

- **Multidisciplinary research approaches need to be explored.** Health promotion research could benefit from a team approach combining the expertise and perspectives of different academic disciplines: for example a behavioural psychologist, a medical sociologist or a medical anthropologist, with nursing and medical expertise.

- **Cost-benefit analyses need to be built in to large trials.** Methods need to be developed to assess the costs to patients (for example the time taken to attend health checks and the economic costs of modifying the diet), as well as service costs. The economic evaluation of interventions should be built into the trial rather than 'tacked on' to the end.

- **Large trials should include an analysis of the harmful effects of screening.** For example, screening may confer a false sense of security or may cause unwarranted anxiety over risk factor levels.

- **The dissemination of research results and the implementation of findings should be built into the funding of major trials.** There is a need for researchers and medical journalists to work together to ensure that results are reported accurately through the media and to primary care team members. The reporting of results also has implications for the motivation of the primary care team. Since good quality data cannot be collected in a vacuum, feedback of results is vital for future studies. The resource implications, including clinical and managerial time in implementing the research findings, should be researched and included in the reporting of trial results.

- **Trusted opinion leaders should communicate to relevant health care professionals the results of health promotion research studies.** This could form part of the planned dissemination process.

Topics for future research

- **There is a need for further policy research.** This should include:
  - Models assessing the impact of fiscal change.
  - Assessment of the cost-effectiveness of existing interventions.
  - The opportunity costs and disbenefits of screening.

- **Further research into the epidemiology of CHD is needed.** There is a need for a better understanding of the interaction of risk factors and the relative importance of stress, different types of physical activity, diet, cholesterol and social inequality.

- **There is a need for RCTs and/or observational studies in the following areas.**
  - An RCT comparing family and individual intervention strategies.
  - A comparison of opportunistic advice and mass screening programmes.
  - A comparison of different models of behavioural change.
  - Perceptions of risk in different populations.
  - How to effect dietary change.
  - The value of cholesterol screening.
  - Why children *do not* smoke. Most children try cigarettes at some time, but not all continue to smoke.
  - How to effect change in young people, particularly through the effective use of the school environment.
  - Why some people do not attend or drop out of health clinics.
  - Effective methods of changing behaviours, and why some lifestyle messages are effective and others are not.

- **There is a need for further research on improving practice.** This should include research on:
  - Models of effective teamworking in primary care. This would include the relative skills and strengths of team members, and models for the best use of these skills.
  - The effect of the health behaviours of GPs and other primary care team members on the message being conveyed.
  - Effective methods of professional education.

- Where and how patients and service users would like to obtain information.

This section is based largely on the reports of two expert meeting workshops on Implications for research. *The workshops were chaired by Dr Steve Gillam and Dr Sally Kendall and reports were written by Dr Lesley Rogers and Dr Mike Rayner.*

Health promotion bands

The following sets out the content requirements of the three health promotion bands, as defined in *GP Health Promotion Package: Guidance on Implementation (1993)*.

BAND 1

Aim
To develop a practice age-sex register, ascertain smoking habits in the practice population and offer advice and appropriate interventions to reduce smoking.

Objective
Ascertain relevant information on the target population (people aged 15-74) at an appropriate coverage level and carry out appropriate interventions, concentrating on priority groups within the target population.

Services
(i)   Collect information on age, sex and smoking status.
(ii) Offer advice and other appropriate interventions and follow up, taking into account relevant local factors and following practice guidelines.
(iii) Focus on identified priority groups, ensuring measures are taken to reach those in priority groups not presenting at the surgery.
(iv) Work jointly when appropriate with other individuals or agencies to further the aim of the programme.

---

* See footnote on page 5.

BAND 2

Includes the content of Band 1

Aim

To minimise mortality and morbidity of patients with hypertension, coronary heart disease (CHD) and stroke.

Objective

Carry out a programme designed to identify relevant patient groups and to minimise the risk from raised blood pressure (BP) and the risk of CHD/stroke.

Services

(i) Seek out undiscovered raised BP by means of regular checks of the target population (people aged 15-74) at an appropriate coverage level.

(ii) Maintain a register of patients with hypertension, CHD and stroke.

(iii) Manage these patients in accordance with practice guidelines by means of lifestyle interventions wherever appropriate.

(iv) Work jointly when appropriate with other individuals or agencies to further the aims of the programme.

BAND 3

Includes the content of both Band 1 and Band 2.

Aim

To reduce the incidence of coronary heart disease (CHD) and stroke by a programme of primary prevention.

Objective

Ascertain relevant information on the target population (people aged 15-74) at (an) appropriate level(s) of coverage and carry out a programme of lifestyle interventions for those found to be at risk of CHD/stroke, concentrating on priority groups within the target population.

Services

(i) Collect information on: smoking; blood pressure; body mass index; alcohol consumption; family history (where appropriate); and monitor diet and physical activity in the target population.

(ii) Offer advice and other appropriate interventions and follow up, taking into account relevant local factors and following practice guidelines.

(iii) Focus activity on priority groups and ensure measures are taken to reach those in priority groups not presenting at the surgery.

(iv) Work jointly when appropriate with other individuals or agencies to further the aim of the programme.

Reproduced from FHSL (93) 3. *GP Contract Health Promotion Package: Guidance on Implementation.* January 1993.

List of participants

Dr Ashley Adamson, British Dietetic Association
Ms Janet Bailey, Association of Facilitators in Primary Care
Dr Ian Baird, British Heart Foundation
Mr Ian Bashford, Scottish Office, Home and Health Department
Dr Kathie Binysh, Department of Health
Ms Jeanette Boobier, Practice Nurse
Ms Lisa Bullard-Cawthorne, National Heart Forum
Ms Margaret Buttigieg, Health Visitors' Association
Dr Alistair Cameron, National Health Service Executive, Department of
   Health
Dr John Chisholm, British Medical Association
Dr Angela Coulter, King's Fund
Dr Sarah Cowley, Department of Nursing Studies, King's College
   London (Health Visitors' Association)
Ms Joan Curzio, Department of Medicine and Therapeutics, Gardiner
   Institute, Western Infirmary (nurse researcher)
Dr Sheelagh Davidson, Health Education Authority
Dr Christina Davies, Medical Research Council
Dr Tony Dowell, Centre for Research in Primary Care
Dr Yvonne Doyle, Faculty of Public Health Medicine
Ms Marilyn Eveleigh, East Sussex Family Health Services Authority
   (nurse adviser)
Ms Linda Ewles, Avon Family Health Services Authority (health pro-
   motion manager)
Ms Anne Ford, Practice Nurse Forum, Royal College of Nursing
Dr Godfrey Fowler, Department of Public Health and Primary Care,
   Oxford University, (OXCHECK)
Ms Atie Fox, Practice Nurse Forum, Royal College of Nursing
Dr Simon Fradd, British Medical Association
Mr Nick Freemantle, National Health Service Centre for Reviews and
   Dissemination

Ms Elaine Fullard, National Primary Care Facilitation Programme
Dr Steve Gillam, Department of Public Health, Bedfordshire Health
Dr Judy Gilley, British Medical Association
Dr Alan Glanz, Department of Health
Ms Susan Gooding, Health Education Authority Primary Health Care Unit
Ms Margaret Gosling, Practice Nurse, Leeds
Dr Muir Gray, Anglia and Oxford Regional Health Authority
Ms Gina Higginbottom, Health Visitors' Association
Ms Paula Hunt, Health Education Authority Primary Health Care Unit
Professor Marie Johnston, Department of Psychology, University of St Andrews
Professor Desmond Julian, National Heart Forum
Dr Sally Kendall, Faculty of Health Studies, Buckinghamshire College at Brunel University (nurse researcher)
Ms Amanda Killoran, Health Education Authority
Professor Ann-Louise Kinmonth, Primary Care Medical Group, University of Southampton, (British Family Heart Study)
Dr Tim Lancaster, Department of Public Health and Primary Care, Oxford University, (OXCHECK)
Ms Susan Le Touze, Research Fellow, Centre for Health Service Studies, University of Kent
Ms Rosie Leyden, Wordworks
Ms Sarah Luft, English National Board
Dr Adrian Mairs, Department of Health and Social Security, Northern Ireland
Professor David Mant, Department of Primary Care Epidemiology, University of Southampton
Professor Michael Marmot, Department of Epidemiology and Public Health, University College London
Dr Theresa Marteau, Psychology and Genetics Research Group, United Medical and Dental Schools of Guy's and St Thomas' Hospitals
Dr Alan Maryon Davis, Health Promotion Subgroup of the Public Health Network
Professor Klim McPherson, Health Promotion Sciences Unit, London School of Hygiene and Tropical Medicine
Dr John Muir, Department of Public Health and Primary Care, Oxford University, (OXCHECK)
Dr John Noakes, Royal College of General Practitioners
Ms Jean O'Brien, National Health Service Executive, Department of Health
Ms Aislinn O'Dwyer, North West Regional Health Authority

Professor Michael Oliver, National Heart and Lung Institute

Ms Clare O'Neil, Nursing Study Co-ordinator, (OXCHECK)

Dr Roisin Pill, Department of General Practice, University of Wales College of Medicine

Dr Steven Platt, London School of Hygiene and Tropical Medicine

Dr Vivienne Press, Department of Health

Dr Roger Ramsay, Royal College of General Practitioners

Dr Mike Rayner, Department of Public Health and Primary Care, Oxford University

Ms Bridget Riches, National Health Service Executive, Department of Health

Professor Lewis Ritchie, Department of General Practice, University of Aberdeen

Dr John Robson, Healthy Eastenders Project

Dr Lesley Rogers, National Heart Forum

Professor Gerry Shaper, Royal Free Hospital School of Medicine

Ms Chris Shearin, King's Fund

Ms Olivia Simmonds, Association of Facilitators in Primary Care

Dr Viv Speller, Wessex Regional Health Authority

Ms Martine Standish, Society of Health Education and Health Promotion Specialists

Professor Nigel Stott, Department of General Practice, University of Wales College of Medicine

Dr Kieran Sweeney, GP, Research Fellow, Exeter University

Mr David Thompson, National Institute of Nursing

Dr Simon Thompson, Department of Medical Statistics, London School of Hygiene and Tropical Medicine, (British Family Heart Study)

Dr Margaret Thorogood, Health Promotion Sciences Unit, London School of Hygiene and Tropical Medicine

Dr David Todd, National Association of Fundholding Practices

Mr Chris Totten, Society of Health Education and Health Promotion Specialists

Dr Tim van Zwanennberg, Newcastle and North Tyneside Health Commission

Ms Heather Waring, British Heart Foundation

Ms Valerie Weeks, Department of Health

Ms Sue White, National Health Service Executive, Department of Health

Professor David Wilkin, Centre for Primary Care Research, Manchester

Dr Hywel Williams, Welsh Office

Ms Fedelma Winkler, Kent Family Health Services Authority

Mr David Wonderling, Department of Health Economics, Brunel University

Dr David Wood, Regional Adviser in General Practice

Professor David Wood, National Heart and Lung Institute, (British Family Heart Study)

Ms Lesley Wyman, Health Education Authority Primary Health Care Unit

Ms Joanne Yarwood, Nursing Studies Co-ordinator, (British Family Heart Study)

Dr Pat Yudkin, Department of Public Health and Primary Care, Oxford University, (OXCHECK)

Printed in the United Kingdom for HMSO
Dd301515 12/95 C50 G559 10170